A Guide to Children's Spelling Development

for Parents & Teachers

by
Mary Tarasoff

Active Learning Institute
Victoria, B.C.

Copyright © 1992 Mary Tarasoff

World rights reserved. No part of this publication may be stored in a retrieval system, transmitted, or reproduced in any way, including but not limited to photocopy, photograph, magnetic or other record, without the prior agreement and written permission of the author.

Canadian Cataloguing in Publication Data
Tarasoff, Mary, 1944–
   A guide to children's spelling development

   ISBN 1-895111-02-1

   1. English language—Orthography and spelling—Study and teaching. 2. Spelling ability. I. Title.
   LB1574.T37   1992   372.6'32   C92-091204-4

Published in Canada by:
   Active Learning Institute
   P.O. Box 6275
   Victoria, B.C. V8P 5L5
   Tel: (604) 477-0105
   Fax: (604) 477-9105

Table of Contents

List of Tables v

Preface vii

I   What is Spelling? 1

II   What is Involved in Learning to Spell? 9

III   Preparing the Way: The Beginnings 23

IV   Using Letters and Sounds to Construct Spellings 33

V   Moving On: Letter Sequences Related to Sounds 61

VI   Expanding the Spelling Vocabulary: Multisyllabic Words . . . 71

VII   Beyond Letters Related to Sounds: Spelling Related to Meaning 77
- Contractions
- Compounds
- Capitals
- Possessives
- Homonyms
- Root Words and Endings
- Root Words and Suffixes
- Root Words and Prefixes
- Combining Forms

VIII Spelling Strategies Children Can Learn 99

- Evaluating Children's Spelling Strategies
- Self-concept
- Develop Listening, Speaking and Reading Vocabularies
- Develop Interest in Words and in Finding Common Spelling Patterns
- Write Frequently
- Be willing to Construct Spellings Based on What You Know
- Use Chanting (Spelling in Rhythms) and Knowledge of Rhyming Words
- Use Mnemonic Devices
- Learn to Visualize words
- Learn How to Proofread
- Use Knowledge of Letter-Sound Relationships
- Use Knowledge of Letter Sequence-Sound Relationships
- Use Knowledge About Spelling Patterns in Syllables
- Use Knowledge About Root Words, Endings, Suffixes, Prefixes and Combining Forms
- Use Knowledge About Word Origins

IX Annotated Samples of Children's Writing 117

- Evaluation of Spelling and Suggestions for Helping

Appendices

A. Growing and Learning: Focus on Writing 143

B. Words that can be Used to Teach Phonetic, Sounding-Out, and Word-Analogy Strategies 149

C. Frequently Used Words 161

D. One Child's Development Over One Year 165

Tables

Table 1	Consonants and Consonant Combinations	5
Table 2	Vowels and Common Vowel Combinations	6
Table 3	Letter Sequences Used to Represent Vowel Sounds	7
Table 4	The Knowledge about Spelling that Children Learn	12
Table 5	Common Letter Sequences	16
Table 6	The 115 Most Frequently Used Words	46
Table 7	Sound and Letter-Sequence Relationships	68
Table 8	Developmental Trends	69
Table 9	Contractions	81
Table 10	Some Compound Words	83
Table 12	Patterns for Adding Inflectional Endings	88
Table 12	Commonly Used Prefixes and Suffixes	92
Table 13	Spelling–Sound/Patterns for Adding Suffixes	94
Table 14	Common Roots and Combining Forms	97
Table 15	Words Spelled Using Different Strategies and Knowledge	100

Preface

You can certainly hit a tennis ball without lessons from a professional. Also, you can improve your stroke by watching more experienced players. However, you will improve even more by getting specific pointers from someone who has more experience and understanding about tennis skills. Becoming aware of and focusing your attention on specific movements or actions will have a direct effect on improving your swing. Without some instruction, you may attend to extraneous movements that don't have a direct impact on improvement.

Once you have received some instruction and tried intentionally to change, it is only through experiencing and doing (rather than just understanding) that improvement takes place. By using a new stroke, it becomes your normal swing. Through repetition while playing tennis, it becomes internalized and no longer requires careful attention and effort. No longer does the stroke need to be "constructed," or thought about, each time. So it is with spelling.

You can point out spelling patterns and strategies to children, you can help them focus their attention and efforts on spelling words. To really help them you need to ensure they are choosing and enjoying frequent writing activities. Without this, spelling has no functional use and does not become an integral part of the writing process.

This book is a guide to children's spelling as well as a guide to how children learn. Many of the principles are the same as for other learning. This book is for parents and teachers because both need to understand how children learn spelling. If you have reasonable expectations and help children be successful, you will help them become competent spellers while also enhancing their willingness to become enthusiastic writers.

To understand how children develop as spellers, you need to have a general understanding of the function of spelling, the common patterns of the English language, and the strategies that children use and can learn to use. This book will help you understand why children spell words as they do and what you might do to help them develop spelling skills as they become writers.

The knowledge, skills and attitudes presented in this book are applicable to all children. It is recognized that children are individuals with different patterns of growth. Learning spelling appears to come naturally to some, and with great effort to others. Understanding what spelling really is and how children learn it will enable you to help all children, whatever their needs.

In this book you will find ways to help children learn the strategies that are best for them. You will learn how to focus their attention on spelling patterns and help them learn how to study words. Children with special needs can also learn the same things, but instructional pace and progress will vary, as it does for all children. Become a learner with your child, become curious about words, search and discover patterns in spelling, and become aware of how spelling is really learned.

Use this book as a guide. It provides you with the understanding to know how and when to encourage, to answer questions, to sit back and watch, to provide guidance, or to celebrate your children's progress.

1
What is Spelling?

Spelling is only one aspect of communicating through written language.

A child's discovery and use of language, through exploration and experimentation, is an individual and creative, yet persistent and purposeful journey. Learning to communicate through language involves listening, speaking, reading and writing. Learning to spell is only one aspect of developing written communication. In fact, spelling becomes important only in the process of sharing written communication with others. Correct spelling makes reading easier because it enables any reader to more quickly recognize words. The reader's attention then can be given to understanding the ideas rather than to figuring out words. What else is involved in learning to be a writer is described in Appendix A.

The main purpose for helping children become good spellers is to help them become willing and competent users of written language.

This book will help you understand how children learn about spelling and how to help them work through the process. It is essential you keep in mind that encouraging children to express themselves and their ideas in written form is the primary goal. Once the ideas are written down, spelling can be corrected.

Too much focus at first on perfect spelling may discourage children resulting in avoidance of writing activities.

If children have spent much time and energy memorizing spellings and correcting errors but never wish to write, their spelling skills will not be used. Too much attention at first on correct form and spelling may dampen their desire to write. Once children are confident and eager to write, once they have learned about language sounds and letters, and once they have had satisfying experiences attempting to write down ideas and stories, then they will be ready to focus on spelling and correct form while continuing to develop writing skills. It is important to stimulate rather than stifle development and to help children learn without removing their own initiative.

Spelling is writing down ideas and words which actually represent objects and thoughts. By using symbols to represent speech sounds and words, spelling freezes speech and ideas into writing which can be read by others. Learning to spell correctly makes writing, and reading that writing, easier.

Patterns governing spelling:

letter and sound

letter sequence and sound

spelling and meaning

The letters used in spelling sometimes closely match the sounds in words (**b a t, f ou n d**). Other times the sound is related to a particular letter sequence (sta**tion**, tex**ture**). Still other times spelling is related to meaning. For example, *they're, their* and *there* sound the same but their different spellings indicate different meanings. Also the same spelling of the root word *view* in *viewing, review, reviewed* and *interview* or *sign* in *signal, insignia* and *insignificant* indicates that the words are related in meaning.

Spelling is more than memorizing the sequence of letters in each word. It involves recognizing patterns of letter sequences related to speech sounds and meaning. Sometimes these patterns can be traced to the word's history rather than to the sounds in words.

> **There are only a few *rules* that exist without exception for writing words in English:**
>
> **1) q is always followed by u**
>
> **2) words do not end in v or j**
>
> **3) every syllable must have one vowel sound**

During the evolution of the language, words from many other languages were included in the English vocabulary. Word origins often explain a particular spelling. A word like *night* reflects the way it was pronounced at the time it was first used in books published on the first printing presses. Many words reveal their Greek, Latin, French, German or other origins, reflecting the diversity of languages that influenced the development of the English language. Over the centuries, a few rules governing the English writing system developed, such as:

1) **q** is always followed by **u**

2) Words never end in **v** and **j** (**ve** and **ge** are used for these sounds)

3) Certain combinations of letters are possible (**spl, ght, ou, ea**) others are not (**qps, lkh, ao, ouw**)

Rules also govern how letters representing sounds can be combined into syllables. These rules vary for different languages. For example:

1) In Hawaiian, each syllable must have one vowel, or one consonant and one vowel: *hula* (**hula**), *aloha* (**aloha**).

2) In English, a syllable must have one vowel sound and may have one, two or three consonants before and after the vowel sound: *str i ngs, tr a p, m ea t, t oy* or *h ou se* (the **e** is silent). Note that a vowel sound can generally be represented by one or two letters (**a, e, i, o, u, y, ee, ea, ou, ow, aw, oi,** etc.) or a *vowel* plus silent **e** marker (**plane, joke**).

4 A Guide to Children's Spelling Development

Consonants may be combined to represent new sounds.

If there are three consonant *sounds* at the beginning of a syllable, the first will be an **s** (as in **spl**ints, **spr**ing, **str**oke). But what about words like Christmas or throw? They don't begin with an **s** and they have three consonants. Although that is true, there really are only two consonant *sounds*: **ch** and **r** or **th** and **r**.

Some consonants occur together but represent a sound that is different from the sounds of the individual letters. These letter combinations are called consonant digraphs, for example, **th** (*think, this*), **ch** (*chop, choir*) and **sh** (*shape*). The digraph **wh** (*whale*) is included in this group because it used to have a sound that could be distinguished from **w** (*wet*). Some consonant digraphs are blended with **r** (*three, shrimp, Christmas*).

Some consonant sounds may be blended together

Other consonant combinations blend their individual letter sounds rather than change them. These are called consonant blends. They can be grouped as follows:

- l-blends (**bl, cl, fl, gl, pl**)
- r-blends (**br, cr, dr, fr, gr, pr, tr**)
- s-blends (**sc, sk, sl, sm, sn, sp, st, sw, scr, spl, spr, squ, str**) (see Table 1)

Some consonants have 2 sounds.

Some consonants may have more than one sound. For example, **c** and **g** have a soft sound (/**s**/ and /**j**/) when followed by **i, e** or **y**, and a hard sound (/**k**/ and /**g**/) when followed by **a, o** or **u**. Some words with the soft sounds are: *city, cent, fancy, giant, gentle, gym*. Some with the hard sound are *cat, cotton, cut, gate, goat, gum*.

Although there are only 26 letters in the alphabet, the 40 to 50 speech sounds found in English are represented by using letters individually and in combinations.

Therefore, by using letters alone as well as combining two or three letters together, the 40 to 50 sound units of English can be represented with the 26 letters of the alphabet.

In addition to consonants being used together to form new sounds (consonant digraphs), two vowels can represent one sound (vowel digraphs): **ai, ay, ee, ea, oa**. In these cases the sound is that of the first vowel. Other vowel combinations (called diphthongs) result in new vowel sounds, for example: **ou, ow, oi, oy, au, oo** (see Table 2).

One vowel may be used individually or with others to represent different sounds. As well, different letter combinations may represent one sound.

Besides a letter being used with others to represent several sounds, one sound may be represented by different combinations of letters. When a vowel has a sound the same as its letter name, it is said to have a long vowel sound. During the evolution of English, the letter **e** was often placed at the end of a word to signal the long sound of the previous vowel. This **e**, used as a long vowel marker, is silent. Thus words ending with a vowel and a consonant (*cap, hop, cut*) have short vowel sounds. Adding **e** signals that the vowel will have

Table 1 Consonants and Consonant Combinations

Consonants	b c d f g h j k l m n p q r s t v w x y z	Blends	bl cl fl gl pl br cr dr fr gr pr tr sc sk sl sm sn sp st sw scr spl spr squ str
Consonant Digraphs	ch sh th wh		

Table 2 Vowels and Common Vowel Combinations

Vowels*	a e i o u sometimes y
Vowel Digraphs	ai ay ea ee oa
Diphthongs	oi oy ou ow oo aw au ew
R-Controlled Vowels	ar er ir or ur

* w is sometimes included because it combines with other vowels as in n**ew**, h**ow** and l**aw**

the long vowel sound (*cape, hope, cute*). In this way the combination of **vowel + consonant + e marker** frequently indicates a long vowel sound (vce pattern).

The same long vowel sound may also be represented by different letters. For example, common patterns for the long /ā/ sound are **ai** (*rain*), **ay** (*day*), **a_e** (*whale*). Less common patterns are **ea** (*great*) **ei** (*weight*) and **ey** (*convey*) (see Table 3). Although this seems to make English spelling unnecessarily confusing, it allows more meaning to be conveyed through print. For example, in reading *nose* and *knows*, you do not need an entire sentence to understand which meaning is being referred to.

Children learn these patterns as they write words and become curious about spelling. Acquiring an extensive spelling vocabulary requires many years and, in fact, continues throughout a person's life. There are specific patterns that children can learn at certain times; for example, they generally can begin with one syllable words having two or three letters. The first words that children can learn to spell correctly are those that have one letter to one sound relationships (cat, dog, pat, it,

Table 3 Letter Sequences Used to Represent Vowel Sounds*

Short Vowel Spelling Patterns

short a /ă/	_a_ hat				
short e /ĕ/	_e_ pet	ea head			
short i /ĭ/	_i_ pit	_y_ gypsy			
short o /ŏ/	_o_ pot	al ball	au sauce	aw saw	wa water
short u /ŭ/	_u_ but				

Long Vowel Spelling Patterns

long a /ā/	a_e cake	ai rain	ay play	ei weight	ea great	ey convey
long e /ē/	ee feet	ea seat	y party	ey hockey	_e me	ie field · ei receive
long i /ī/	y my	igh night	i_e kite	ie pie		
long o /ō/	o_e home	oa boat	ow snow	_o go	oe toe	
long u /ū/	oo school	u_e cube	ew new	ue true	ou soup	ui fruit

Other Vowel Patterns

ou ow	out how
oo	good look foot
oi oy	join boy
r-controlled	ar or er ir ur air are ear ear car for her stir fur hair care earth bear

*the most common patterns for each sound are listed first

go, and, me) and words that they use often (to, my, the) or want to know (mom, dad, love, Santa). Later they learn words that contain blends and digraphs (trap, crab, this, ship) and those that have vowel patterns (each, house, how). Adding endings correctly to words and spelling multisyllabic words are generally learned later as they write, read and learn even more. Appendix B gives lists of words that have these patterns.

❖ ❖ ❖ ❖

Fee-Fi-Fo-Fum siad Bigelow when he was walking down the road to his houes to eat some soup then he went to Mrs. pimberly to give some soup

Draft

Written by an 8 ½-year-old.

In this sample note that many correctly spelled words have letter sequences related to sounds (*down, when, road, then*) as well as one letter related to one sound (*his, went, he*). Words that do not follow regular phonic patterns (*walk, some, Mrs. was, soup*) are also correctly spelled. These are often referred to as "sight words" and indicate that the child is probably relying on visual image. The spellings of **siad** (*said*) and **houes** (*house*) also suggest that the child knows the correct letters, but doesn't yet have a clear visual memory of the spellings.

What is Involved in Learning to Spell?

Spelling is important in making writing, and reading that writing, easier.

Spelling is important only as a convention for putting words and ideas on paper so others can read them easily. If no one other than the author reads the writing, conventional spelling is not essential. Taking notes can be made faster if the writer invents abbreviations for frequently used words, thus creating a personal shorthand. However, it would be difficult for another person to read these notes because this constructed spelling system would not be familiar.

Conventional or standardized spelling are other terms for correct spelling. These terms reflect the fact that correct spelling is only an agreed upon way to represent speech sounds and meaning.

Spelling facilitates the writing process because conventional, standardized or correct spelling (as it is variously referred to) makes reading easier. Thes mens thit reding iz mor difekalt ef wun es nat femelyr wef thut ritr's sestm fr ripresntng wrdz. You can read these words, but not as quickly as when they are correctly spelled. Trying to read these words is similar to listening to speech that is mumbled or spoken with an unfamiliar accent. It takes more effort and more time to figure out the message.

The function of spelling in the writing process and in the reading process is different. In writing and spelling, each letter has to be recalled from memory; in reading, a word just has to be recognized and its splng dos nt hv t b cmplt n ordr to rcgnze the word in sentences. During the reading process, grammar, meaning and

In reading, the word only has to be recognized. In spelling, each letter needs to be recalled in sequence.

background knowledge help the reader predict and recognize printed words. Therefore, children may be good readers without knowing how to spell all the words they are able to read. However, they cannot be expected to accurately spell words they have never heard before or cannot read.

Knowledge and skills are developed and refined as they are used.

Attitudes towards learning grow out of one's interests and successes.

All learning involves refining and expanding prior knowledge. Everyone acquires new knowledge by relating it to what they already know. For both children and adults, knowledge and skills are refined and developed as they are used. It is easier to remember things that you want to learn, that pose a problem you need to solve, or that you feel make sense. Similarly, learning to spell is made easier if you are curious about the language and its spelling system, if you can build on what you already know, and if you have an interest or need to spell words. You are generally more willing to pursue those activities that you do successfully and enjoy.

As an adult, it is difficult to retrace your own learning path, particularly at the early stages, because you do not remember how you learned. As a result, it is often difficult to understand how children learn to spell and what it is they need to learn.

Spelling is not rote memorization of letter sequences.

Spelling is not just a matter of rote memorization of the letter sequences in each word. Children eventually learn to spell 50,000 to 60,000 words, but certainly not by studying each word in school. Typically in 10 school years only about 3,000 to 4,000 words are presented in spelling lessons. Even these 3,000 to 4,000 words are not necessarily learned from these lessons, or are perhaps learned and forgotten. Also, which of about 600,000 words that can be found in a dictionary should be taught and memorized?

What is Involved in Learning to Spell? 11

What do you need to learn in order to be able to spell?

Look at the following passage and think about what you need to know in order to determine if the words are spelled correctly.

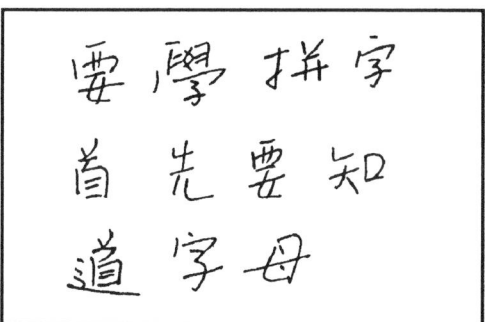

What you need to know about the writing system is:

- How to make the marks (letters)
- Which way to write (right to left, left to right, bottom to top)
- How the marks represent sounds (letter-sound relationships, or phonics)
- How the marks represent meaning (letter sequences often represent meaning rather than sound)
- How letters are grouped to represent words (concept of word), sentences (punctuation) and thoughts (paragraphs)

The spellings of unfamiliar words are constructed using a variety of strategies. More familiar words are written from memory with little thought required.

Table 4 illustrates the kinds of knowledge children gain about spelling over the years. As children develop spelling skills they use what they know to **construct** spellings, moving from a focus on letters and sounds to visual and meaning cues. At first young children have to construct most spellings because they are not familiar with words and often can't read the words they want to write. Through writing and reading activities they become more familiar with letter patterns and the look of words.

Table 4 The Knowledge about Spelling that Children Learn

Listening and Speaking Vocabularies
- develop as children interact with others and the world

Control of Writing and Drawing Implements
- develop as children make marks on paper, using pens, pencils, crayons, computer keyboard

Awareness of Print
- they learn about letter names and letter forms
  - children draw letters on paper—scattered, left to right, right to left

Letters Represent Specific Speech Sounds: One to One Relationships
- letter chosen to match letter name heard
- letter chosen because articulation of its sound matches articulation of letter name
- letter chosen to represent letter sound (phonics)
  - consonants and short vowels used to match articulation or sounds of letters

Letter Sequences Related to Sounds: Beyond One to One Relationships
- children use consonant digraphs, consonant blends, vowel digraphs, diphthongs, and other patterns

Letter Sequence Patterns in Multisyllabic Words
- syllables represent parts of spoken words
- every syllable has a vowel sound (1 or 2 vowels)
- spelling of sounds in syllable sometimes have patterns different from those in one syllable words
- endings, prefixes, suffixes form syllables

Letter Sequence Patterns Related to Meaning

contractions	endings
compounds	suffixes
homonyms	prefixes
root words	combining forms

Expanding Spelling Vocabulary

What is Involved in Learning to Spell? 13

Gaining a knowledge of language through listening and speaking lays the foundation for reading and writing, and also for spelling.

Children's spelling begins with the development of oral language skills gained through listening and speaking. This provides the basis of their understanding of the function of language and develops the vocabulary which they will call upon in their writing. Children cannot be expected to spell words correctly, if they have not heard them, cannot pronounce them and cannot read them. However, they can begin to write their ideas down by using what knowledge they have about letters and sounds to construct spelling. Through these beginning attempts, they learn about spelling.

With an emerging awareness of print, young children become curious about letters and words seen in their environment. Along with this awareness, preliminary spelling involves learning how to print letters, how to talk about them (their letter names), and about the sounds they represent. In order to learn about printing letters and letter names, children need to be able to control and manipulate writing tools (pens, pencils, crayons, etc.). With the increasing availability of computers in homes and schools, children also have opportunities to learn about letters and spelling by becoming familiar with the computer keyboard and software.

Children begin to become aware of letters and to realize that print carries meaning.

In the beginning stages children figure out the basis of language: (a) the form of written language (letters and the relationship between the letters and meaning and sound) and (b) the function of written language (print carries meaning). They begin to realize that the story read from a book is contained in the print, not in the pictures, and that they can transmit their thoughts by writing letters together in certain ways. Often they will copy words they see, even though they don't know what they say. They will learn by memory how to print their name, sometimes without knowing the letter names because they have memorized the shape of the letters.

Children begin to realize that letters are combined in sequence from left to right. At first, these look like random letter sequences.

By participating in discussions, by listening to stories and by talking with peers and adults, children's speaking and listening vocabularies continue to grow. With this increasing awareness of spoken language and an increasing control of printing skills and knowledge of letter names and sounds, children attempt to print and write messages. In this writing, using printing or computers, they produce strings of letters which represent messages.

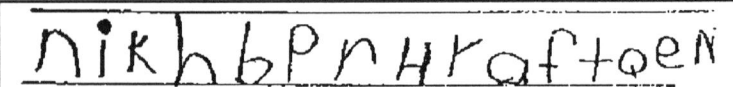

My grandma bought me a blanket and some dishes.

Learning more about letter-sound relationships, children use this knowledge to construct messages with words that have the correct initial consonants and the letters that sound like their letter names.

Gaining an increased awareness of letter-sound relationships, children become able to use their knowledge of letter forms, letter names and speech. To write short messages they begin to sound out words. Written messages that used to be seemingly random letter sequences begin to contain words represented with correct initial consonants and perhaps some final consonants, for example:

"ddonmmetsgklsp" becomes "i lv m d"
(*I love mom and dad*)

What is Involved in Learning to Spell?

As children learn and experience more, they spell words using initial and final consonants. Gradually they become more aware of vowels and begin to include them also.

With continued efforts and experiences, children spell more sounds with the correct consonants. Vowels, although not necessarily the right ones, begin to appear in approximately the correct places (fon = fun). At this time children are using their knowledge of letter-sound relationships: one letter for one sound. This results in spelling that can be read using a phonics approach. The message is no longer a seemingly random sequence of letters.

However, most English words do not have one letter to one sound spelling patterns. Therefore, this first strategy that children use needs to be refined by the realization that sounds are also represented by letter sequences (a few letters representing one sound). Some of the patterns learned first are:

- **ch, th** and **sh** represent sounds not related to the individual letters,
- **ee, ea, y** and **cy** can all represent the long /ē/ sound
- **ou, ow** can represent the same sound
- **igh** represents the long /ī/ sound
- **ck** (*pick, flock, shack*) is used at the end of words, not just **c** or **k** (**pic pik, floc flok, shac shak**)
- **wor** (as in *word, worst, world, worth*) sounds like *were*

(See Table 5 for other patterns.)

Children can learn about letter sequences–sound relationships. They can begin to recognize common letter sequence patterns.

Later, when their writing vocabulary includes more multisyllabic words, children need to become aware of the spelling patterns in syllables. The spelling of sounds in syllables differs from their spelling in one syllable words, for example: *picture* not **pickture** and *table* not **taybull**.

Children also learn that some of the common syllables are not spelled the way they sound, for example:

nation not **na**shun
adven**ture** not adven**cher**

With experience writing, over time children become quite able to apply their knowledge of these patterns to construct the spelling of an increasing number of one syllable words. As their listening, speaking and reading vocabularies expand so does the number of words they attempt to spell.

Table 5 Common Letter Sequences

wor-	*world work worm worth*
-nk	*bank honk pink sunk*
-ng	*hang song wing stung*
-ck -ke	*quack* (short vowel sound) *quake* (long vowel sound)
-ce -se	*voice race* (ce sound like /s/) *nose phase* (se sounds like /z/)
ef el em en es ex	— sound like their letter names: f l m n s x , **cū** sounds like q, **wī** sounds like y, **cā** sounds like k
-dge -ge	*badge edge bridge dodge fudge stage huge*
-tch -ch	*batch fetch ditch clutch rich each*
silent letters	-b (*thumb*) -gh (*night, high*) h- (*ghost*) k- (*knee*) w- (*write*) -n (*column*)
-age	*village bandage advantage damage*
-tion	*station mention fiction*
-ture	*picture nature adventure future*
-ic	*picnic attic*
-le	*rumble battle title*
-ia -ious **-ian -ier** **-iest -io**	*India curious* *Victorian funnier* (i sounds like /ē/) *happiest radio*

Eventually they can learn about stressed and unstressed syllables (not all syllables are pronounced with the same emphasis). Multisyllabic words can't be spelled correctly by sounding out each syllable. The vowels in unstressed syllables generally have a sound that is called the *schwa* sound rather than the expected long or short vowel sound. In the word *syllable*, for example, the **a** has the schwa sound, not the long /ā/ or short /ă/ sound. In the dictionary this sound is represented by the symbol /ə/.

In the beginning children at first focus on letters and their relationship to sounds. However, because many words in English have spellings that relate to their meaning or origin rather than strictly to their sound, spelling strategies need to change. When children have had more experience with spelling, they are able to understand this added dimension and to use a variety of strategies.

As spellers become more competent, they also rely more and more on visual strategies and meaning-spelling relationships.

Awareness of the connection between spelling and meaning completes the understanding that spellers need to acquire. Some meaning-spelling connections are:

- The different spellings of sound-alike words to represent different meanings (homonyms, or homophones, such as *rain, rein, reign; son, sun*)

- The **ed** ending to indicate the past tense, (i.e. the action is finished) is always spelled the same despite its different sounds (as in *planted, skipped* and *answered*)

Gradually as their vocabularies expand, children develop a bank of words that they can write from memory. This means they don't have to construct the spellings each time.

- Words or roots to which prefixes are added maintain their spelling: **mis** and **spell** become *misspell*, **re** and **establish** become *reestablish*

- The spelling of the root remains the same although its pronunciation may change slightly with the addition of a suffix; sometimes these changes help in remembering the spelling of related words, for example: *sign—signal, define—definition, compose—composition*

This book is a guide to the journey children take as they learn to become writers. It provides a map with viewpoints describing children's spelling development. Not all children travel the same path. Some travel faster than others along certain legs of the journey; others begin later but might arrive down the path at the same spot at the same time. Some parts take longer than others. You are probably well aware that children learn to sit, walk, speak and read at different ages and that most children do acquire these abilities. The precise age of acquiring an ability is not as important as ensuring that children do gain the knowledge and skills at some point and that they want to continue to learn and to write.

Some children have particular needs because of individual physical, emotional or cognitive attributes. These children can benefit from finding which strategies, as suggested in this book, help them learn best. Presenting spelling in an organized way by clearly illustrating the patterns and relationships will also enhance their learning. What needs to be learned and the general hierarchy is the same for all children. However, the rate of learning and the way of remembering spellings will differ for each child.

Throughout the learning process children need encouragement, support and appropriate guidance. If you know about spelling patterns and strategies and understand the stages children grow and learn through, you can provide the additional support and guidance for your children to become competent, confident and enthusiastic writers.

Learning to spell is connected to acquiring competency in all language skills.

The following sections give the highlights of how children develop spelling skills. The kinds of words children attempt to spell relate to their listening, speaking and reading vocabularies. Because spelling is a way of writing down language, it is not an isolated subject; its acquisition is connected to learning other language skills. The way children spell words indicates what they know about the language and its spelling.

It involves, not rote memory, but active thinking.

When children learn, they use creative and critical thinking skills in solving problems. So, too, with spelling. Children figure out how language works and how it is represented on paper. For example, they must discover relationships between words, letters, sounds and meaning. They need to figure out how to remember spellings. Because there are too many words to memorize each word individually, children need to learn strategies for organizing, sorting, generalizing and constructing spellings. This very active process involves much more than rote memorization.

By studying how children learn to spell, researchers have identified general trends common to different ages of children and grouped these into developmental stages. These stages help clarify what children are doing. Some stages will not be noticed in some children—perhaps they did not go through that stage, it went unnoticed, or it was very short. Characteristics of one stage will be mingled with those of other stages. Children also reach the various stages at different times. This is why they are called developmental. The unfolding is related to their physiological and intellectual development. Children are able to do certain things only when they are ready. For instance, they cannot walk at two months of age because the necessary muscular development has not yet occurred.

Becoming a competent speller is a process that occurs over time and is related to developmental learning patterns.

> Once a developmental stage has been reached, then guidance and feedback can help children learn more easily. Helping them learn involves knowing what to expect and when to provide help.

Learning a new skill is difficult at first. When we say children have difficulty, we generally mean the following:

- They do a task in, what seems to us, an awkward way
- They need a lot of guidance (coaching)
- They tire easily in comparison to someone who competently performs the skill

This is normal in learning. Learning involves a period of difficulty or challenge because it involves gaining mastery over something new. With each attempt children learn a little more, then one day they perform the task without help. Over time, their proficiency continues to increase. Beginning too early to expect the end

Learning new skills and knowledge presents challenges and difficulties. Active efforts are needed. At first, skills are awkward and knowledge is imperfect. With continued effort and use, they become more refined and accomplished.

result can produce frustration in both children and the adults who are trying to help. Beginning too late to develop certain skills may imply the skills are not important. Not introducing skills that could be developed may delay their acquisition.

When children are not ready to master a skill, you can at least model the skill, provide them with experiences, and discuss what is involved. In this way, they can become aware of what they might eventually want to learn. For example, young children watching older people use handwriting instead of printing want to do the same and try to imitate the writing as best they can.

Effective teaching means children learn. If you feel they are not learning, then perhaps the methods, challenges or expectations need to be reassessed. You may need to look more closely to see what learning is occurring. Maybe you have not seen what they have learned. Perhaps you wanted them to learn something else or something that is too difficult at this time.

The following points are important in facilitating children's learning:
- Ensure they feel successful and that they view their improvement as success even though there is still more to be learned
- Provide experiences and help them meet challenges that are within their reach
- Help them believe they can and will learn by pointing out what they have learned rather than stressing what they don't know.

Evidence of what children know about spelling is gained by examining their writing, and listening and watching as they write. Evidence of their growth or progress is seen by comparing samples and observations of their writing over time. Saving samples of children's writing and drawings, and making notes of what they said or asked when they were writing or drawing provides a chronicle of their journey over the years. You will be able to view the rough spots, peaks, turning points and overall progress towards the end goal.

> **It would be impossible to say when any one person knew or could do all that is possible, even in one specific area. The more you know, the more you realize you don't know.**

There is no absolute time limit or magic age for reaching a particular goal. However, it is important that there is continued progress towards the goal and that children maintain their desire to keep learning. How often have you set a goal for yourself and then, upon achieving it, realized that there was still more to learn in order to become more proficient? It is difficult to define the point at which you can say there is nothing more to be learned or improved. Rather, it is a matter of deciding what degree of competency you wish to have.

Learning is continuous throughout life. It is impossible to live without learning (whether you want to or not). What you actually can do is make choices about what to learn or not learn rather than whether or not to learn.

III

Preparing the Way: The Beginnings

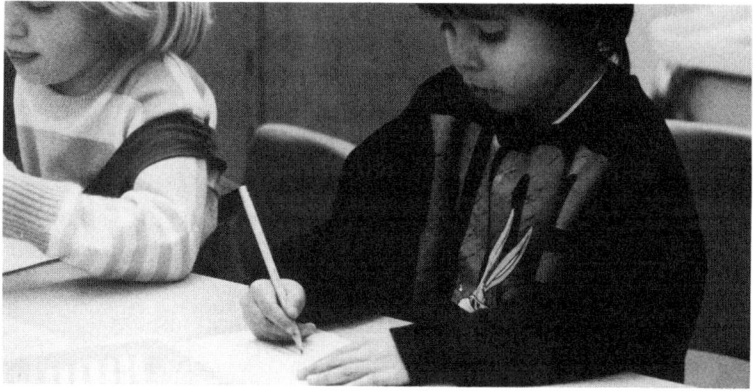

Young children draw lines and squiggles at first. They learn to make marks on paper and control writing implements. Some even are compelled to write on any surface such as a wall or table. They will also imitate the way others write. So when writing, they make wiggly lines because that is what the writing appears to be. If a computer is available, children will press certain keys and imitate the keyboarding process producing strings of letters.

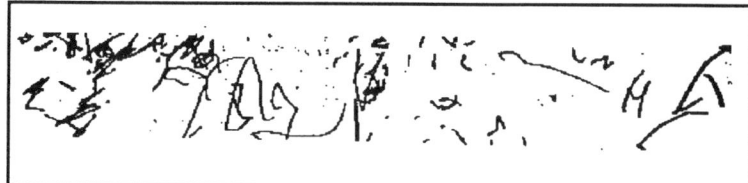

Later, letter-like squiggles appear in these marks, perhaps accidentally at first. When this occurs with children who are becoming aware of print in their environment and in stories read to them, they may attempt to draw the letter forms again and ask about these letters. They learn by watching their friends, siblings or adults print or write.

No message is represented by the letters. In these initial drawings, they are part of the picture. Some children seem able to print the letters in their name, but when asked to spell their name (name the letters), they falter. They are, in fact, drawing the letters as if they were shapes composed of lines. They do not think of each letter as a symbol with a name. As a result, letters may be drawn sideways, backwards or upside down. You may notice extra lines in the letters (₣ for **E**) or lines not quite joined (/ϙ for **b**).

"It's a drawing.
That's me.
That's money."

While children are attempting to draw and print, they are gaining better control over the implements and learn to draw circles, squares, diagonal lines, lines that cross, triangles, shapes that join together and so on. This progress is evident in their drawings and printing. On a computer keyboard they are becoming faster locating and identifying letters.

Preparing the Way: The Beginnings   25

This picture was drawn after listening to a story. The child is able to represent people in the drawing. When asked what he would like to say, the child responded, *"I am going to wait 'til the tide is down."* He has something to say, but not the skills to begin writing it down.

This child is developing more control of drawing and provides more details in the figure.

"I went to the beach."

"I am driving a race truck."

His name is printed with letters close together (as a word). Notice the use of a capital letter to begin the name and lower case for the other letters.

At this very beginning stage, to help you can:

- Provide paper and drawing implements (pens, pencils, crayons) and opportunities for your children to use them, both on their own and with you working at their side. If you have a computer, let them experiment with pressing keys and observe the effects. Computer software programs that present alphabet games and drawing programs may stimulate their interest.

- Notice development in their control of the implements progressing from drawing wiggly lines, squiggles and dots to making circles, straighter lines, to making squares, rectangles, "corners," triangles, diagonal lines and crossed lines. It is interesting to keep a few samples as your children grow and learn.

- Listen to children as they draw. Often they are talking to themselves about their drawing. Or ask them to tell you about the picture after they have finished. This is the beginning of representing thoughts on paper. You may find out that what looks like random marks actually has meaning.

- Provide other experiences with print. Read to your children, point out signs, labels, names. Talk about the letters in words. Make letters with playdough, in sand, on paper. Make messages with magnetic letters or write notes and read them to your children.

- Let them see you write, read and respond to written messages. This is called modeling. It is a powerful way to help children learn without formally teaching them. In fact, much of what children learn is acquired through watching and imitating others, especially people they like and admire.

- Let them help you make grocery or chore lists, or "write" a reminder or a letter to a relative or friend. By doing this children begin to understand that print can be used to transmit meaning. It is important to let children write or type messages even though the messages do not look like print.

Often one of the first words children want to print is their own name. They may also be interested in learning to print mom and dad, as well as their siblings' and friends' names.

Note the relationship between the printing of her name (above) and the writing (below). This child is aware of the left-to-right linearity of print. She is able to name only the letter **J**. The other letters are shapes without names. The print below was done confidently and quickly and in the end became flowing lines.

Her name on top.
"I forgot," in the middle.
"The alphabet," on the bottom.

The letters Justin printed from left to right in a line. A capital letter is used for **J** and lower case for the other letters. The **s** and **n** reflect the difficulty children often have with learning to print these shapes.

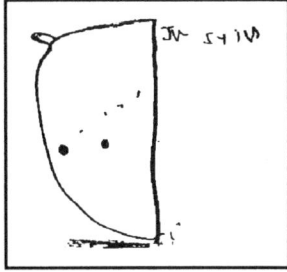

"This is a house and this is the grass and this is—I forget."

- You can help them learn to spell their name by printing or using magnetic letters and saying the letter names. If they are able to print letters, you can print their name (saying the letters as you do it) and let them trace or copy it. Don't use all capital letters. For example, instead of *JOHN* use *John*. Often children will be able to learn only one or two letters at first—perhaps choosing the first and second, the first and last, or only the familiar ones. With further attempts, other letters will be added. Similarly, with a computer keyboard, help them identify the letters, or keys, they want.

- When you print words for them, use lower case letters so they will experience words as they occur normally in printed text and messages.

28 A Guide to Children's Spelling Development

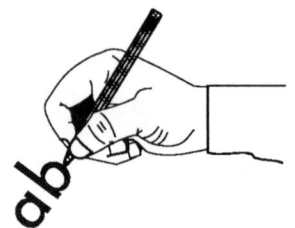

Guidance in printing can be given when children start asking how to make letters. Show them how to form letters as a unit rather than as a series of lines and perhaps describe the action, for example: start at the top, go around, up and down. Making the letters as shown below also prepares children for handwriting. Many printed letters are very similar to handwritten ones if done this way, for example **d** and *d*, **m** and *m*, **p** and *p*.

If children are ready to learn printing, they will attempt to do as you suggest. If not, let them continue to do what they can, approximating the letters as closely as they are able. Be patient and willing to demonstrate ways to print at a later date. One day they will be ready and do it the way you show them.

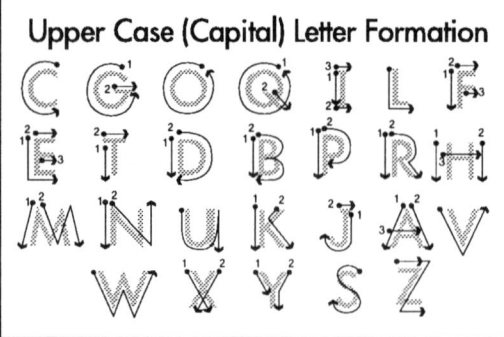

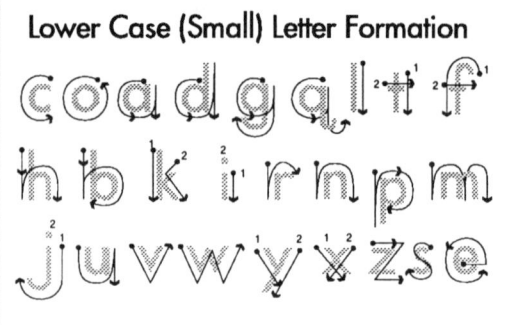

- It may help to have children trace your letter models a few times, then attempt to print letters with their eyes closed. This helps them focus on the movement involved.

- Capital letters are often easier for children to learn. Fewer of the capital letters are confused with each other in comparison to lower case letters, for example: b—d, B—D. However, children need to become familiar with both forms and especially the lower case letters. They need to relate capitals to lower case forms easily so they will recognise that **Go** and **go** are the same word. Also, print that children are exposed to uses mostly lower case letters.

- In helping children learn about letters, name the letters as you print words so letter names will be associated with the printed letter. When you read books you can ask them to find the letter that begins their name or point out the same letters that begin mom, dad or other words they are interested in.

- Play alphabet games: "I spy a letter that begins—(e.g. Katie, John)." "How fast can you find the letter?" You can use magnetic letters, letters printed on cards, story books, magazines and so on.

- Use the Alphadeck card game (available from Active Learning Institute, Box 6275, Victoria, B.C., Canada V8P 5L5). It is a fun way to help your child learn letter names and sounds, and different letter forms.

- As children become able to print or type letters and draw pictures, ask them to tell you about their message, story and/or picture. You might describe something you notice in the picture or comment, "Those look like letters, what do they say?" From their response you will learn whether the letters are objects in the drawing or a message.

- Continue to read books, signs, recipes, notes and so on to your children. Have them near to the print so that you can casually point to words and comment on letters and sounds some of the time.

- In activities when children are writing and drawing, write and draw alongside them, modeling the process of writing and reading messages. Point to the letters while you read. This helps children realize the words you are saying are in the print.

- Talk with children about their experiences and also share your own. Through discussions, children learn to use words with meaning. They increase their speaking vocabulary which will later become the basis for their writing. They also learn how to pronounce words, a skill that can help later with spelling.

- Provide children with a variety of experiences (going to the beach or museum, shopping, playing games, visiting people and places) and read to them. These activities provide children with opportunities to learn about the world and books. From these they gain ideas for writing and develop a sense of written language.

Drawings of pictures and letters begin to occur together. The letters might be part of the picture or they might be an attempt to tell a story or to describe the picture.

"This is Superman. He is saving people."

The following two samples indicate that sometimes children who have been learning to print their names use the letters in their name to print a message about their picture.

Letters accompanying the drawing indicate the understanding that print is a series of letters in lines. The letters used are mostly from his name (Adam). These are the ones he is learning to print.

"It is a sea. There are turtles in the pond."

Similarly, Michael has learned to print his name and uses those letters to represent a message.

"Somebody lived by the water. They swam in the water."

When children realize letters and words carry meaning they begin to print letters (or type messages on the computer) and ask, "What does this say?" or comment that "This says...." The letters accompanying their drawing intend to convey a message or a comment about the picture. This indicates their awareness of the difference between drawing and printing.

> It is normal for young children to print letters, words and entire messages backwards. This is a natural part of learning about letter symbols. The reversal of words and entire messages fades quite early, but reversals of some letters may persist until age 8 or 9.

Individual letters may be reversed or the entire string of letters written completely backwards starting from the right rather than the left. In observing children's writing realize this is a normal part of learning about letters and printing. It takes experience and time for children to learn that letter orientation and direction of printing matter. For some children this happens quite easily and early; others may understand printing occurs from left to right but still have difficulty with the correct orientation of certain letters. Often letters that children continue to reverse are those similar to other letters (such as **p, b, d, q, g**). With experience in writing and examining print and with feedback from others, children can figure out which way letters need to be oriented.

Reversals of letters in words often continue until about age eight or nine. At this age if children who are still reversing some letters are asked to find the letters they printed backwards, they can correct them. Now that they are older and more experienced, these children need to be reminded to monitor their work themselves and self-correct as they print. They need to learn it is important to print letters correctly and not to rely on others to point out the reversals.

NOTES

IV

Using Letters and Sounds to Construct Spellings

According to how they think print works, children begin to systematically use letters to represent phrases, words and word parts. They try to figure out the rules for writing words. For example, they may think the number and size of letters must represent the size of the object or length of the utterance. In the beginning, letters are strung together in what seems to be a random sequence. Often they use the few letters that they know and repeat them. This changes when they learn to print more letters and examine print more closely. Then they may use a variety of letters without many repetitions and they may copy words.

❖   ❖   ❖   ❖

Draft

"This is a beach. It is too windy so they planted some flowers."

This message is printed using letter shapes that the child is becoming aware of. Note the shape of **s**: an extra loop at first and reversed in the second line. This is a difficult shape for children to learn. Letters represented are mostly capitals.

34 A Guide to Children's Spelling Development

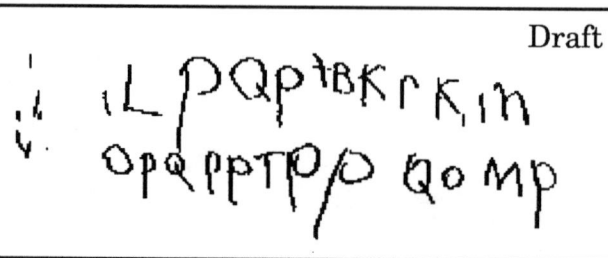

Strings of letters are written to represent a story about a picture. The writing indicates the letters that the child can print.

In this string of letters there is repetition of letters as well as letter sequences (it looks as if the word *today* may have been copied twice). The child seems to be aware of periods in books and writing.

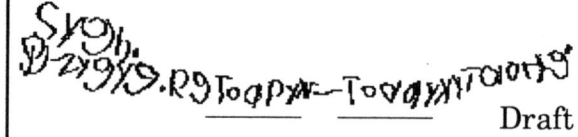

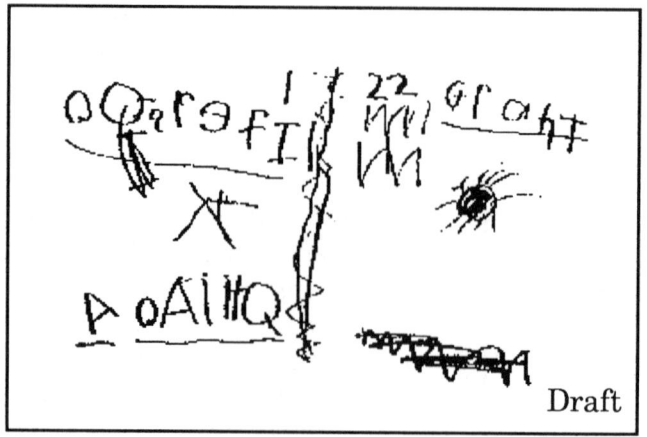

"All I did was just copied from the alphabet. The sun. It's hot."

In response to being asked to write about a story, this child copied letters from the alphabet displayed in the room, and included a drawing of the sun and his name.

✣   ✣   ✣   ✣

Using Letters and Sounds to Construct Spellings

Children attempt to write down their ideas, even though they may not know what the words say. Later they begin to print words (e.g. their name, *mom, dad, love*) they have memorized as a result of printing them many times in their own stories or messages.

Children enjoy demonstrating their knowledge and will print a list of words they know beside pictures they have drawn, even though the words may have no relationship to the picture. These activities are self-initiated opportunities to learn about letters and words and to master printing letters. If they are working on a computer keyboard, they are learning about letter sequences in words and beginning to remember where the keys are.

❖ ❖ ❖ ❖

Draft

"This is different colours of the sea and there's a rainbow shining on the sea."

This child has learned how to print some words and adds them to her picture. Note the **M** in *mom*. Joining diagonal lines (as in **M**) is difficult for beginning printers.

This is a list of words the child has learned to print from memory (*yes, no, daddy* and her friends' names). She adds these to her drawing which is about something else.

Draft

"It's a nice and sunny day for you and me. We're standing out in the grass."

The drawing includes words which the child proudly stated, "I wrote these all by myself." He has learned to print from memory: *mom, dad, Nathan, to, Caleb* and a word part, *ing*. He attempts to construct *water* (**witr**) and *tree* (**tea**) which relate to his drawing. Note the mixture of capital and lower case letters.

Draft

Draft

The drawing is accompanied by some letters and words. The child uses random letters (**F U M B D O C Y**) at first to represent the message, then she decides to extend the writing by copying words from the writing centre in the classroom.

The child prints/copies friends' names and *Tigger* to accompany her drawing. Note the mixture of capitals and lower case letters. The letter **s** is printed correctly once and reversed twice.

Draft

Using Letters and Sounds to Construct Spellings

> cornflake leaves hed
> Beth the tree of
> Are they a bird H fast
> or the breeze.
> *Draft*

This is a poem copied during an independent writing time. Note, the letter formation reflects the effort the child makes to copy the letters. In choosing to copy, the child has an opportunity to develop more control of his pencil marks and letter formation. Although unable to construct his own spelling, the child can still learn about letters and written language at his level.

This child first uses a string of letters (**ACOAJBeocKIHelo**), then she finishes the message with spelling constructed using letter names and beginning consonants, **f** is used for **th** in **wf** (*with*). She realizes that words have consistent spellings: **coc** is used each time for *cat* and **paey** for *playing*.

Draft

M paey wf m coc
(*Me playing with my cat*)

I L paey w(?) m coc
(*I like playing with my cat*)

✥   ✥   ✥   ✥

Talking about letters with children when they are involved in reading and writing activities and games helps them learn letter names.

Through frequent writing opportunities children learn to print letters from memory. This is important for learning to spell because they cannot write words easily if they can't readily recall how to print letters.

By watching others read and write, children begin to realize that sounds in words are related to the letters. They begin to pay more attention to sounding out words. They learn more about letter sounds by asking questions as they write and by getting help from others who point out letter sounds (in alphabet books, alphabet games and stories). They use this knowledge to construct spellings. If they continue to become more familiar with letter forms (naming and printing letters from memory), they will be able to combine their knowledge of letters and sounds to help them represent spoken words.

Children who know the names of letters will often realize that some sounds in a word are the same as a letter's name. Therefore, in their beginning spelling, they may represent the word or sound by a letter, for example, **m** for *am*, **u** for *you*, **b** for *be*, **k** for the sound of **ca** in *cape*, **r** for **ar** in *party*. In constructing its spelling, *party* may be represented as **prd** if the word is pronounced as *pardy* or if the **t** is perceived as a /d/ sound. Similarly, *middle* may become **mtl** and *little*, **ldl**.

When children sound out words, they also feel how the mouth and tongue are used in producing sounds (articulation cues). This relationship between articulation and sounds provides another strategy used along with letter names in constructing spelling. The letter whose name is articulated closest to the sound will be used: **h** for /ch/, **k** for /g/, **c** for /s/, **y** for /w/, **t** for /d/, **b** for /p/, **a** for /ĕ/ (as in *pet*), **e** for /ĭ/ (as in *it*) and so on. If you don't know why a word has been spelled in a certain way, try saying the sound and then the name of the letter used. Were the sound and the letter name made in similar ways with the mouth and tongue? Do they sound alike?

Using Letters and Sounds to Construct Spellings

Children use letters that sound like the letter name.

> nO im a brd
> Draft

*No, **I am** a bird.*

> rua car
> Draft

***Are you** a car?*

Parts of the word sound like a letter name, or it seems to sound like a letter name:

> V R o a P B T D P D
> Draft

<u>We</u> <u>are</u> <u>go</u>ing to a birthday par<u>ty</u>.

> I yIT TO the PRK
> Draft

I <u>went</u> to the <u>pa</u>rk.

> A Jr HS
> Draft

A <u>tree</u> house.

tr *is represented by* **jr** *because the sound of* /**j**/ *is made in a similar way to the sound of* /**tr**/.

> tese es the Jragan
> spre Abiwt the fiet
> The Niet pot the Jrae
> IN Jos DAw.
> Draft

*This is the <u>dra</u>gon <u>sto</u>ry ab<u>ou</u>t the fight.
The knight poked the <u>dra</u>gon in his <u>ja</u>w.*

David is attempting to sound out the words *sea* and *snake*. The sample also includes *the*, a word he has learned to spell. Words appear more in a list, than in a line.

"It says, 'David's sea snake.'"

GESRLWKN represents *Geese are walking*. The child constructs spelling by using letter-name strategy: **e** in *geese*, **R** for *are*, **N** for *ing* in **WKN** (*walking*). The child also knows phonics relationships for **G, S, W, K**. Note that there are no spaces between the words.

GAAtN(?) Geese are walking

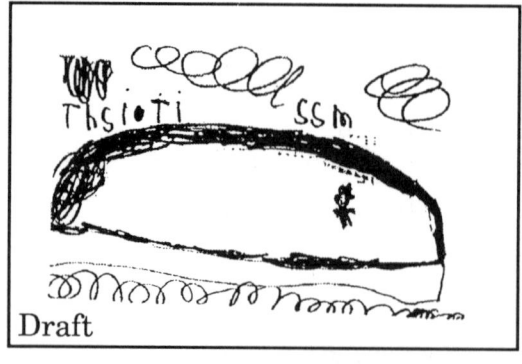

This is a hotel. This is me.

Using letters that he can print and the sounds that are the most obvious, this child has written **ssm** which represents *this is me*. Similarly **Th si otl** represents *This is a hotel*. This indicates that the child knows letter names and some letter sounds; he may even know the /**th**/ sound.

Using Letters and Sounds to Construct Spellings 41

This child has learned to spell *the* and the *ing* ending. She uses letter-name strategy for *are* (**R**) and **o** in *rainbow* (**Rbo**). She also uses one letter for each sound she perceives in the words: **brs** (*birds*), **n** (*in*), **rbo** (*rainbow*).

Draft

The birds are flying in the rainbow. The child told the rest of her story, "The girl can't go flying because there's too much birds in the air so she swings on a swing. She pretends that she's flying in the air."

Draft

I am at the beach today and I'm going to build a sandcastle today.

This child is using a combination of strategies:

• Letter sounds (note that these are initial and final consonants): BD for build and sc for sandcastle

• Known words (*at, today, go, to*) indicate visual memory is being developed

• **TAE** for *the* and **ANG** for *and* also indicate attempts to remember spelling visually

✢   ✢   ✢   ✢

In the beginning, writing is limited by the child's fluency in printing and spelling words on paper. It requires much energy. What children write does not reflect their thoughts. Rather it reflects their present knowledge of spelling and their ability to easily write words on paper.

Children at this point in their progress may be using four strategies to construct the spelling of words:

- Random letter sequences
- Sounding out using letter names and letter sounds
- Articulation cues
- Words they have memorized because of frequent use or interest.

Children are able to understand very concrete and obvious relationships at first (the sound of /ā/ in *play* is written as **a**). With further development they become more capable of understanding increasingly abstract ideas. One of these more abstract understandings is that a letter may represent a certain sound not related to its name or articulation. This is the beginning of an awareness of sound-symbol relationships, or phonics. For example, with the word *came*, they begin to realize **km** is not the spelling and begin to write **cam**. They can understand that two letters **c** and **k** have the same sound and that although /**ca**/ in this word sounds like **k**, it is spelled **ca**. Later they can understand that the silent **e** is needed to mark the long vowel sound.

With more experience, children produce messages in which the use of phonics can be seen. They use correctly those consonants that they are the most familiar with. Usually these are the sounds made similarly to their letter names and those most frequently used. They generally find the sounds of **b, t, s, m, n, p, d, z, k, j, f** and **c** easier to learn than **r, g, h, l, w, v, x, y** and **q**.

You may also note that as children experiment with print and are involved in many writing activities, they learn to spell frequently used words correctly and easily. They are beginning to memorize spellings, not by practising them (for example, in a word list), but by using them over and over in their own writing. Both motor (printing) patterns and visual images of words are being established because the words are being printed and seen many times in the writing they have chosen to do.

As well as using words they have memorized through frequent use, children should continue to construct less familiar words using their knowledge of letters and sounds. Even adults continue to do this. For unfamiliar words (those that are new or not used frequently), adults construct spellings based on what they know about words. Having more knowledge and experience than children, these constructed spellings are often close to the correct spelling. After generating a few alternatives, more experienced writers can choose the one that looks right, or, if still undecided, can look in a dictionary. Being able to construct a reasonably close spelling also helps when using a computer spell checker. If the spelling is not fairly close, the computer cannot provide the needed word.

This message is readable because either the words have the conventional spelling or are represented closely by phonics. The child is aware of the **ch** and its sound. The **Re** for *are* indicates that the child uses a letter-name strategy for the /**r**/ sound. It also indicates he is becoming aware of correct spelling so adds an **e**. The **t** in *water* is perceived and written as **d**, and the /**er**/ sound is represented by **r** (**WaDR**). The use of **a** in **WaDR** may indicate that the child is beginning to establish visual image of correct spelling.

Draft

It is the beach. The fish are swimming in the water. The child also wanted to write: "They're at the beach playing in the sand. You can go swimming and you can make sandcastles. These are clams and crabs."

Draft

The child said, "The butterfly is flying." And she wrote, "The bird is too. They're friends."

This child is using phonics relationships to represent each sound she perceives (**BRD, thr, Frans**). From frequent writing, *the* and *to* are correctly remembered. **ni** is used instead of *is*. This indicates that the child knows *is* and *in* are similar and has confused them this time. Also, it might be a writing error.

✧   ✧   ✧   ✧

Knowing that children use these strategies and knowledge about letters and words, you have a starting point for helping them at this point in their development.

- Encourage children to sound out the words they want to use, and to print the letters they think correspond. This helps them use the knowledge of letter sounds they have already acquired. Accept what they do. Point out how to use letter name and articulation cues more effectively. You may model the process of sounding out words by saying them slowly but naturally. Don't drag out the sounds to the point that they are distorted and it seems as if two or three letters would be needed to represent the sound. For example, for the word *print*, if the **pr** sound is stretched out they may think it should be spelled **pu er** (**pu er int**).

- Even when you help them, don't insist on all letters being included. Help them write the most obvious sounds they perceive or hear. At first, their spellings may have only the consonants and vowels that sound like letter names. Initial sounds of words are represented first, with final consonants generally coming later.

- Middle consonant sounds, blends and correct vowels can be pointed out as children learn more about writing and spelling. For example, the word *print* in the beginning may be constructed as **p** and later as **pt**. When children become aware of vowels in words, **pet** would be acceptable. Later **pit, prit** or **pint** and eventually **print** will be spelled. Build on what they know, rather than pointing out all the errors.

- If your children are interested, you can point out the correct spellings of some of the words frequently used in their writing. Often the words they memorize first are those such as: *go, to, the, love, I, like, at, is, it, can, and, my, me*. See Table 6 for a list of the most frequently used words.

46 A Guide to Children's Spelling Development

Table 6 The 115 Most Frequently Used Words

like	can	I	it	is	go	me	mom
dad	love	look	at	a	the	see	no
yes	my	and	to	in	you	come	little
went	big	day	do	will	up	here	name
that	on	as	are	of	or	your	how
out	does	saw	with	his	they	have	by
said	into	him	three	he	be	one	had
what	if	has	her	did	say	was	this
from	not	but	all	then	she	now	want
for	we	an	which	them	more	make	off
sister	were	when	there	each	two	may	long
brother	about	many	some	so	these	would	other
could	than	first	been	its	who	people	made
over	down	only	way	find	very	after	just
where	most	know					

Also see Appendix C for a list of 385 more frequently used words.

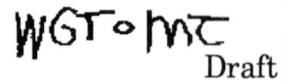

WGTo MC Draft	iNSATNGS Draft	SP N EK Draft
We're going to make jelly.	*I was at my Grandma's.*	*Superman is good.*

Using Letters and Sounds to Construct Spellings 47

As already mentioned, when first beginning to write words and sentences, children tend to run all the letters together in a line. They gradually become consistent in printing the letters from left to right. Some reversals of letters may still occur and this may continue until they have firmly established a basic spelling vocabulary.

At first, letters are strung together in a line. Spaces between words appear once children become aware of this concept.

In speech, the sounds of words are not clearly separated. However, the conventions of writing and spelling separate words in print. Spaces between words appear when children develop a consistent concept of what a word is (where a word begins and ends). This idea seems quite obvious to you because you have had many experiences with written language. You are not even aware it was something you had to learn before you could read and write. Children gain this awareness through their writing and reading experiences in which they become aware of initial and final sounds of words. At some point, spaces, dots or lines appear in their writing to separate words.

Draft	Draft
MI B Is H	My G____ and G.____
	R am to V____t

My brother is home.   *My Grandma and Grandpa are coming to visit.*

The spelling used by beginning writers is often referred to as *invented* or *developmental* spelling. Actually a more useful term is *constructed* spelling. Children construct spellings of words based on the knowledge and strategies they have learned. Their spelling reflects what they know and how they use that knowledge.

At this point in their development, you can:

- Ask your children to point to a word or to write a word. Children who have not gained awareness of this concept will point to a sentence, a group of words, a letter or even numbers, or they may print several words together. To help them learn about words, print a sentence that they tell you on a strip of paper. Cut apart the words and help them reconstruct the sentence. With other sentences on strips, let them cut the words apart. Have fun making up new or funny sentences.

- Notice in their writing that only a few vowels (unless they sound like the vowel's letter name) are included at this time. Vowels in words are generally more difficult to hear or to feel when articulating words. They will appear in children's writing when the representation of initial and final consonants is well developed.

- Notice that **m** and **n** before consonants (for example, *want, ring, jump, bank*) are not easily heard or felt in articulation and so do not appear in children's writing until later.

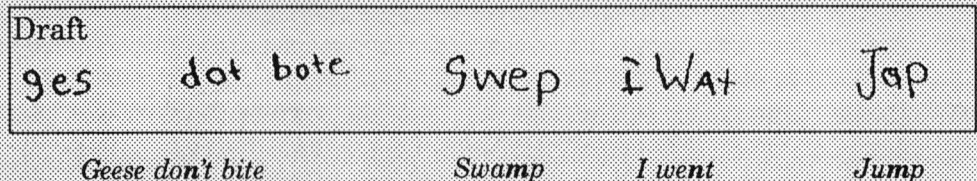

Draft				
ges	dot bote	Swep	I WAt	Jap
Geese don't bite		*Swamp*	*I went*	*Jump*

- In helping children learn to spell, encourage the natural learning process by answering their questions about spelling. Encourage them to decide which consonants to use. Do not insist on them sounding out all the sounds in the words, but help them put down as many as they perceive. You can show them the correct spelling, especially if they ask, perhaps saying "You have spelled it the way it sounds. This is the way it is spelled in books. There is another letter here...." Do not expect every word to be correct in the beginning. Correcting every word will discourage rather than encourage progress.

Using Letters and Sounds to Construct Spellings

At any one particular time, children are using several strategies and a range of knowledge. These change as children use and learn more about the language. In the beginning stages, the knowledge they have includes:

- Letter names and letter forms
- That sounds (words) and writing are related
- That letters are strung together in a line

Children construct the spelling for words they are not familiar with. They use a variety of strategies which they continue to refine and learn as they write messages and stories.

The strategies used include:

- Random letter sequencing
- Relating sounds to letter names
- Relating articulation of sounds to articulation of letter names
- Relating speech sounds to letter sounds (phonics)
- Copying words
- Printing words they remember because they have written them so often

❖ ❖ ❖ ❖

This child knows how to spell *like, to, play, jump, the*. The other words are spelled using 1:1 letter-sound relationships. **h** is used for **ch** because the sound /**ch**/ is similar to the sound of the name of **h**. The words are well spaced.

> I liKe to woh sels Play
> The JumP otvthe wotr
> Draft

50   A Guide to Children's Spelling Development

Draft

When asked about her writing she said, "Once upon a time there was a little sea urchin that paddled around. He saw whales and he saw rocks and he saw an octopus. He got bitten. That's it."

The child copied a friend (see below). When asked if she as going to finish the story, she wrote, *To mommy and daddy and Leanna. Love from Jackie.*

Children learn from each other. If they are not comfortable with writing on their own or have not developed the skills, they will copy or imitate others—a learning strategy we all use.

Draft

This is a story about Sarah. Once upon a time there was a little girl. Her name was Sarah. The child added when talking about the story, "Sarah saw a rainbow in the sky. She saw the sun." She had printed all she could; time, interest or energy ran out.

Spellings known: *was, this, is, a*

Visually close spellings: **sory** (*story*), **lette** (*little*), **abot** (*about*)

These indicate both phonics and visual strategies are being used. Unfamiliar words are constructed using phonics and letter-name strategies: **thar, nam, grle, opon**. She also relates sounds of words to those already known: **was opon atam** (*once upon a time*). *Was* sounds similar to *once*.

✢   ✢   ✢   ✢

When children are beginning writers, their thoughts are far more fluent than their printing and spelling. Thus drawings and conversations provide easier outlets for conveying thoughts than writing. Children can print only a small amount of what they are thinking. In fact, children's initial writing reflects more about how the child solves spelling problems than the actual thought. They need to use drawings accompanying words to express their thoughts until their printing and spelling skills become more adept. Through speech and self-talk while they draw, they also develop and practise the language skills and vocabulary that will form the basis of their later writing skills.

Continuing to develop and learn, children become aware that between consonants there are other sounds (vowels) and may choose one particular vowel to represent those sounds (perhaps **a** or **o**). Arbitrarily using one vowel, they add this new strategy to the other phonics, articulation and letter name strategies already used.

The first correctly spelled vowel sounds other than those that sound like the name of the vowel itself are the short /ă/ (as in *cat*) and the short /ŏ/ (as in *pot*). The correct representation of the short /ĭ/ (*fit*) and especially the short /ŭ/ (*cut*) and /ĕ/ (*pet*) comes later. Instead of relating the sound to the correct vowel, for **i, e** and **u**, articulation cues continue to be used. This means as children sound out the vowel sound /ĕ/ they relate it to the name of the letter **a**, made with mouth and tongue in a similar position. Therefore, in their writing you will find words in which the following apply:

- **a** represents the short /ĕ/ sound (*pat* spelled for *pet*)
- **e** represents short /ĭ/ (*fesh* for *fish*)
- **a** or **o** represents short /ŭ/ (*fon* for *fun*)

> IwrS GINI
> Draft

I was gonna

> I lake gees tae
> or nos I rile
> lake gees.
> Draft

*I like geese. They are nice.
I really like geese.*

> hr wasa grl
> he laFd bsib
> The beh
> asl h mom he
> he cad go to aF
> The beh hr
> mom sad wa
> tal tre rid
> gogon ad vd
> wecad go to
> The beh kwe
> go to the beh yas.
> Draft

There was a girl. She lived beside the beach. She asked her mom if she could go to the beach. Her mom said, "Wait 'til the tide goes out and then we can go to the beach." "Can we go to the beach?" "Yes."

Phonics knowledge and strategy is indicated by the correct initial and final consonants and the awareness of vowel sounds. This child is using **a** as the vowel to represent many vowel sounds: **lafd** (*lived*), **af** (*if*), **tal** (*'til*), **sad** (*said*). He uses letter-name strategy, when vowel sound is long: **beh** (*beach*), **bsid** (*beside*), **tid** (*tide*).

Articulation and letter-name cues are used: **h** in **beh** represents the /ch/ sound, **f** is substituted for **v** in lafd (*lived*).

he is used for *she* because child may actually be saying "he," or may use **h** to represent **sh.**

Use of visual memory is indicated by correct spelling of *was, mom, go, to, the, we.*

Note: each time *beach* is spelled it is the same, **beh.** Perhaps the child realizes that words have a consistent spelling. So once it is figured out, it only needs to be copied.

✢   ✢   ✢   ✢

To help children develop awareness of vowel sounds and correctly use them in spelling, you can:

- Help them distinguish the initial consonant of words. This helps them separate consonant sounds from vowel sounds and brings awareness of other sounds in words. Have them think of words that begin with the same sound, or identify or draw pictures of words that have the same beginning sounds.

- Play rhyming games, make up rhyming word chants, or read nursery rhymes and leave the rhyming word out for them to say. This helps children become aware of ending sounds and separates the vowel sound from the initial consonants.

- Sort words by vowel sounds. Use either picture cards or words printed on cards. Be sure they can read the words being used. (See Appendix B for examples of words to use.)

- Sort words by rhyme, initial consonants, final consonants, etc. This helps children become aware of the spelling patterns. These activities could be structured as a speed sorting game (challenge the clock) to see how fast it can be done.

- Picture and word cards can also be used to play games like:
  - fish (get two words that rhyme or start with the same sound)
  - rummy (get sets of 3 or 4 pictures that begin with the same sound)
  - memory (turn all the cards upside down and try to locate pairs of a specific kind)

(The Alphadeck Card Game can be used for learning letters and sounds (see page 29). Also, see Appendices B and C for words that can be used.)

> - Watch your children and talk with them as they write. Examine and compare their completed writing with earlier samples. You can then identify changes that are occurring. You will see progression from random letter sequences, to initial consonants; initial and final consonants; initial, medial and final consonants and the inclusions of vowels as markers; and then the correct vowels. Over time you will notice some words are spelled correctly and from memory (sight words). Overall the strategies used change from reliance on spelling words by using letter names, articulation cues and letter sounds (phonics), to spelling using phonics, knowledge of letter patterns and memory.

The underlying principle governing spelling progress is that children use what they know about letters and words to spell. If they have used a word frequently or have a desire or need to know its spelling, it becomes part of their spelling repertoire that can be written without thought to the individual letters. They just know how to spell the word. Other less familiar words are constructed each time using what is known about spelling. The more children learn about the patterns and strategies of spelling and the more they write and get feedback, the more their spelling will approach conventional spelling.

When looking at children's writing, you need to consider many factors before you can feel you know how well their spelling is progressing.

Some questions that should be considered are:
- Was this a subject they were knowledgeable about and had interest in? In other words did they have something to say that they wanted to write down? Quality of response is directly related to this.

- Was this their first attempt to write down their ideas or have they gone back and edited their work?

- What would they change on their own if they were asked to improve their writing?

- How much support was given to them as they worked? Were they able to get help from their peers? What resources were available?

- What were they thinking about as they wrote the words? What strategies were they using? Did they use only words they knew were correct? Did they write letters without matching them to sounds? Did they match sounds to letters in the conventional way? Did they spell words the way they pronounced them?

- What does the sample indicate about spelling? Can you say children who use a string of letters to represent words are spelling incorrectly or are they unaware of spelling? Can you say children who make errors are poor spellers or they don't know enough spelling? How many errors indicate a spelling problem? What kinds of errors indicate difficulty?

- In the spelling they construct, what do the children demonstrate they know about spelling? How much should they know and by when, and why?

- Did you notice what they can do rather than only what they can't? Did you think about how complex their knowledge is even though every word is not spelled conventionally?

Answers to many of these questions come as you begin to understand what is involved in learning to spell. It is not simply memorizing letter sequences. It involves learning about the writing system and how it represents words. It involves becoming aware of letter sequences and patterns, and their relationships to sounds and meanings. It is a learning process that takes place over time, building on what was previously learned and being consolidated through meaningful use. At each stage children are competent spellers if they are using what they know about the letters, sounds and patterns to help them spell. As their listening, speaking and reading vocabularies increase, and their abilities increase with guidance and encouragement, so will their writing and spelling competency.

The range of spelling development seen in the following samples from a group of 5, 6 and 7-year-olds also indicates the stages of development that individual children might go through, from using letter strings to increased awareness of letter-sound relationships and memorizing spelling of frequently written words. The constructed spelling becomes readable using a phonics approach and gradually spelling becomes closer and closer to the conventional.

❖ ❖ ❖ ❖

Six and seven-year-old children wrote responses to a picture of two geese. The samples which follow indicate the range of responses demonstrated by these children on one particular day, to one particular type of activity. It would be very difficult to guess the actual age of each child based on these samples. It would also be impossible to determine exactly what they know about spelling without having been there to observe them working and to talk with them about how they go about spelling words.

Using Letters and Sounds to Construct Spellings 57

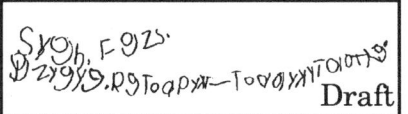

This child understands that letters occur in a linear sequence from right to left. She uses letters that she knows how to print.

The writing demonstrates right-to-left, linear organization with awareness of other writing marks (periods and a dash). The range of letters used is limited.

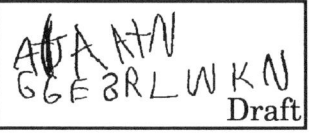

Geese are walking.

The first line of letters is difficult to interpret. Perhaps the child is trying to sound out the names of the geese. In the second line the child obviously is sounding out the words and relating sounds to letters.

This child has named the geese first. Obviously she tries to make changes to the second name. This child, then, chooses to print a message using the correct spellings of words that she is sure of.

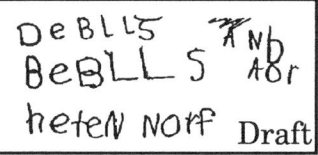

"These geese are heading north."

This readable message is based on phonics. The child may "hear" **t** for **d** in **heten** (*heading*) or the child may actually pronounce it that way (similarly, **f** for **th** in **norf** (*north*)). To find out, you would need to talk with the child.

Phonics knowledge and strategies are used to construct readable text. The child is aware of correct initial and final consonant sounds. Prenasal consonant is omitted in *don't*, **dot**. The spellings of *they* (**tae, hae**), *these* (**tes**) and *fish* (**fih**) indicate the child has not learned the consonant digraphs.

Visual strategies are indicated by very close spellings: **littile, fih, lake, bote** and correct spellings *and, my, to, eat*.

They (**tae, hae**) and *geese* (**gess, ges, gees**) are constructed differently each time—perhaps trying to visually remember the spellings. *Like* is spelled **lake** each time—perhaps it has been memorized this way.

These geese's names are Skoigb(?) and Gigls(?). These geese don't bite. I like my geese. They like to eat little fish. I like geese. They are nice. I really like geese!

Use of phonics strategies are indicated by correct initial and final consonants and inclusion of vowels. He omits the prenasal consonant **n** (**weat**), using **a** instead. Perhaps he knows visually there should be another letter, but cannot remember it.
Visual strategies are also indicated by the correct spelling of *one, day, was, and*.

W-gls(?) and Gegls(?) went for an adventure one day and it was fun.

Conventional spelling is used for words familiar to this child. The constructed spellings of **bekose** (*because*) and **tere** (*there*) suggest use of visual memory as well as some phonics.

> Jijie and wjie are
> looking at the water
> bekose Tere are fish in The water
>
> Draft

Phonics knowledge and strategies are indicated by the correct initial, medial and final consonants and awareness of vowels in words. For vowels, letter-name (**sa**—*they*, **ball kano**—*volcano*) and vowel placeholder (j**a**mp—*jump*, sw**e**p—*swamp*) strategies are used.

The use of **s** for **th** (**sa**—*they*, **sot**—*thought*) could be a speech substitution. Use of articulation or pronunciation cues results in using **b** (*ball kano*) for **v** (*volcano*).

> Fgl and lol wt to a ball Kano Sa Jamp in to the ball Kano Sa Sot in was a Swep Sa Sot a Jaging the NDE
>
> Draft

Fgl and Lol went to a volcano. They jump into the volcano. They thought it was a swamp. They thought of jogging. The end.

Prenasal consonants **n** and **m** are omitted (**wt**—*went*, **swep**—*swamp*). However, there is a prenasal consonant in ja**m**p (*jump*), perhaps because he has a visual approach to spelling this word rather than a phonics approach.

Visual strategies are indicated by the correct spelling of *and, in, to, the, was, -ing* and the use of *ball* for *vol* (the child relates pronunciation to a word already known).

NOTES

V

Moving On:
Letter Sequences Related to Sounds

Children's spelling progress relies not only on beginning to see the relationships between letters and sounds, but also on a continued growth of their listening, speaking and reading vocabularies. These will be the source of words they attempt to spell. These, of course, develop not only as a result of lessons, but also because of experiences and interactions with others and the environment.

As children's vocabularies increase and they need to spell a larger number of words. They begin to realize that the one letter to one sound relationships (as discussed earlier) do not help them spell all words correctly. Instead of looking at individual letters and their sounds, they begin to be aware of other patterns that "look right." They are now able to identify and use the letter sequences, such as **ed, oi, aw, tion, ture**, that occur frequently and to relate them to the sounds or to the look of words. They are developing a visual memory for letter sequences and spellings.

How does one learn or discover these spelling patterns? Many people suggest the English language has little regularity in its spelling system. They cite examples in which one spelling pattern has different sounds, such as in *comb, tomb, bomb*. They point out that one sound can have a variety of spellings, for example, long /**a**/ can be represented by **ai** (*paint*), **ay** (*say*), **a + consonant + silent e** (*plane*), **ei** (*weigh*), **ea** (*great*), **ey** (*convey*). There are many examples of such irregularities. However, there is far more regularity if letter sequences and meaning are considered and not just one letter to one sound relationships. In fact, knowing about letter sequence-sound relationships helps simplify the learning process. For example, rather than trying to memorize each word separately, the sounds of common letter sequences such as **ight** can help one remember how to spell *frighten, lighten, flight, tight*, and so on.

✣ ✣ ✣ ✣

Draft

Written by an 8 1/2 year old.

I was on my way to the space station when I saw a U.F.O. I ran to the space station and got my laser fighter. Blast off! I shot it down and killed the aliens. I was the hero from then on. P.S. This was on mars.

Note the number of words spelled correctly and the control and ease of printing. With the development of these skills, the length of writing increases.

• Phonics knowledge extends beyond 1:1 letter/sound relationships to awareness of letter sequences related to sounds: **ay** (*way*), **a_e** (*space*), **er** (*laser, fiter*), **ow** (*down*), **sh** (*shot*), **th** (*then*), **ff** (*off*), **ll** (*kill*), **ed** (*killed*)

• Uses phonics to sound out unfamiliar words **aleins** (*aliens*), **stashon** (*station*); the child needs to use visual strategy to learn that **tion** sounds like /**shon**/ or /**shun**/

• Visual strategies are evident by many words spelled correctly and the construction of less familiar words: uses *hear* to help spell **hearo** (*hero*)

• Aware of the notation P.S.

✣ ✣ ✣ ✣

Learning to spell involves becoming aware of common spelling patterns.

Anyone can find and learn these common spelling patterns. The first step is being aware that there are patterns. Learning to spell involves classifying and sorting words by these patterns and actively noting similarities and differences in letter sequences, sound and meaning. Probably you already know from your own experience that to learn to spell a new word you do not usually have to sit down and write the word out several times or memorize it by rote. Instead, you learn it by noting patterns, making connections to other words already known, using the word in writing, and making an effort to remember the spelling. Learning results as you connect new spellings with what you already know and use. Everyone has a few words which are difficult to remember, but this is not different from learning other things. If you really want to remember it, then you try to find a way to relate the spelling to something else or to make it unusual or funny.

The dictionary can help, but even it gives alternative spellings for some words.

When in doubt the dictionary provides the final authority. Even then, there are some acceptable alternatives (for example, *colour, color; defence, defense; practice, practise*) depending on whether you decide to use British or American spelling. The dictionary also provides the key to word origins. This is often helpful in explaining why some words are spelled the way they are. Learning about spelling is, in fact, learning more about the English language.

Tables 1, 2 and 3 (see Section I) summarize common letter sequences found in one syllable words. Some of the letter sequences children learn easily at first are consonant blends and digraphs. Later they use other patterns correctly, such as: **ing, qu, ght, ck, nk, ke, ee, ea, ou, ow, oi, oy** and **au**.

Different patterns are often found in multisyllabic words. Some of these patterns are: **tion, ture, ic, age, ing, est, ous** and **ia**. In spelling multisyllabic words, letter sequences, meaning and sounds are important considerations in understanding how words are spelled. These will be discussed in more detail in the next section.

Children cannot be expected to learn to spell words they cannot read.

Every word will not have to be memorized individually or written frequently if there is an awareness of spelling patterns. With knowledge of common letter sequences, many words can be constructed quite accurately and then "proofread" or checked to see if they look right. Alternative spellings can be written and the one that looks correct, selected: **gees, gesse, *geese*; laff, lauf, lauhg, *laugh*;** or **thier, theyr, *their*.** Children can be expected to identify as correct or incorrect many of the words that are part of their reading vocabulary. If children cannot read the word to begin with, then they will not be able to recognize its correct spelling. With many words, especially those less familiar, correct and/or incorrect spellings may not be recognized even though the words can be read.

Spelling is not memorizing letter sequences in words or spelling rules by rote.

These patterns or generalizations are the basis of what were called "spelling rules." The practice used to be one of memorizing a rule (for example, **i** before **e** except after **c**) and applying it to words in a list, whether or not the words were actually used in the children's writing. Often the object was to learn rules, rather than have children understand spelling patterns which would help them become independent learners. Although the kinds of words presented were generally suitable for most children, the method was not particularly inspiring. Often it did not work for many children because spelling was seen as memorizing lists of words and getting them right on the test rather than as a process of writing words so others could read them. The rules were memorized out of the context of writing. This made it difficult to understand how to use the patterns as a strategy for constructing spelling during the writing process.

Learning to spell involves finding common spelling patterns in words. This aids the memory process by helping to make sense out of what might at first seem to be a system without much regularity.

Learning about common letter sequence patterns reduces the amount that needs to be memorized. Seeing these similarities between words actually helps the memory process. Learning about patterns enables students to begin to recognize patterns on their own and to independently learn more about spelling. This learning can occur even when no spelling lists are given or lessons presented.

Studying the words and patterns that children are currently using in their own writing ensures that the level of difficulty is appropriate. In this way motivation and success are assured. The connection between learning about spelling and using it in writing is also quite clear. The need to provide activities and lessons to ensure children transfer spelling words from a list into their daily writing is reduced. Talking about spelling used in their own writing helps children realize that correct spelling in their writing is important.

Some children discover these patterns and develop visual images of words on their own as they write and read. However, helping them become more aware of many patterns and anomalies allows them to make sense of what seems a first glance to be a spelling system without much regularity. If this is done at a time when children are able to understand and incorporate the patterns into their thinking about spelling, this teaching will enhance their progress. This does not mean they will be able to verbalize all the patterns and point out to you what they are doing, but that they can use these understandings in spelling words.

Some children need little help with learning to spell. Others, however, need very specific assistance at different times. You can:

1) Provide many opportunities to write, experiment, copy, watch, and so on. To know how you can help, observe what they are doing and talk with them about their spelling. Once you have an idea of what kind of information and strategies they use, you can encourage them to continue to use what helps the most.

2) Show them additional strategies and other spelling patterns. Think about what you do when you try to learn the spelling of words. Much of this is common sense, for example:

- Point out little words in longer words and relate it to other knowledge: the *princi**pal*** is your **pal**, a *princip**le*** is a **rule**

- Remember spellings by saying the letters in a rhythm: *dau ght e r, miss iss ipp i*

- Make up sentences that tie similar spellings together: "*meat* is what you *eat*," "an *island is land*."

(See Section VIII for a description of different strategies.)

3) Help children engage in writing activities. You can enhance their ability to get the words down on paper by answering their questions about word use and pointing out spelling patterns. Tables 4, 7 and 8 give a very general progression of what children learn as their spelling skills develop. This provides a rough idea of what children know and what might come next, that is, how to help them learn successfully. It does not mean that you will have children memorize the patterns or practice spelling words in a list by printing them over and over.

4) Talk about the words they need to spell. Show them the correct spelling, have them write it once or twice from memory and perhaps review it a few times over the next few days. This will help them focus on spellings that they do not remember easily.

5) Teach them how to study words independently. Have them do the following:
- Print and say the word
- Decide on the best way to remember it (Section VIII describes several strategies)
- Cover the word
- Print the word again (may need to try 2 or 3 alternative spellings)
- Proofread it (look back and check each letter)

To remember the spelling some children may need to say each letter out loud or silently. Some may want to visualize it. They may want to decide which part of the word is causing them difficulty and focus on that part. Or they may relate it to other words, put it in a sentence with related words, make up a riddle about it or mispronounce it, for example, say the silent letters as in *k nife*.

6) Print words with several similar spelling patterns on cards. Sort the words according to vowel sound, similar endings or similar beginnings. This helps children focus on letter sequences and their sounds.

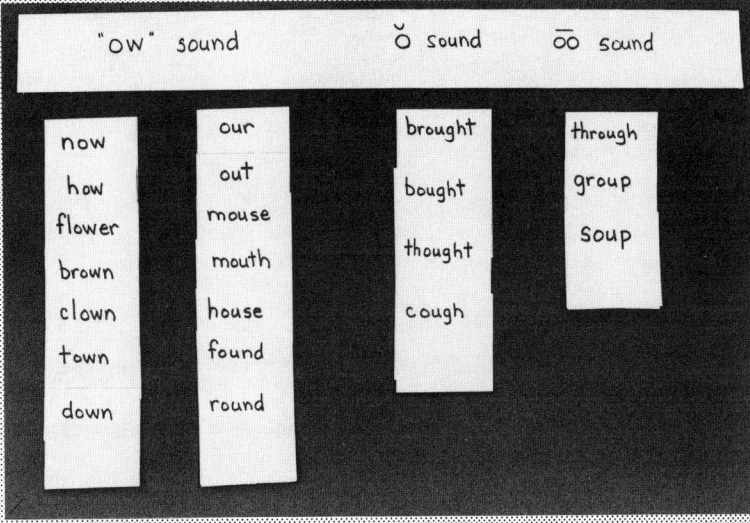

Table 7 Sound and Letter-Sequence Relationships

(To be used as a teaching resource for spelling, not to be memorized by children)

Letter Sequence-Sound		Morphology
consonants b c d f g h j k l m n p r s t v w z	short vowels	
digraphs (ch sh th wh) qu y x	long vowels ai ay ee ea oa	-ing -s
		-ed
blends bl cl fl gl pl br cr dr fr gr pr tr sc sk sl sm sn sp st sw scr spl spr squ str	silent **e** pattern y as a vowel	contractions compounds
-ll -ss -ff	ar or er	-er
-ck -ke -nk -ng		-est
	oi oy ou ow oo	
hard and soft c hard and soft g		irregular plurals
	ir ur ear are	
kn- wr- -ight		possessives capitals
ph gh	au aw ew ie ei	syllables
		affixes root words
-le -tch -dge -tion -ture -age -ia -ier -ious -iest -ian	schwa /ə/	hyphens abbreviations combining forms more irregular plurals assimilated prefixes

Table 8 Developmental Trends

Knowledge	Squiggles Letter-like forms Strings of letters Directionality inconsistent	Initial consonants Initial and final consonants Initial, medial and final consonants Vowel markers and consonants Directionality established Spaces may appear between words Some "sight" words	Short vowels Essential sounds represented Letter sequence-sound correspondences Blends, consonant digraphs Long vowel patterns Words easily read phonetically Spaces between words More "sight" words Some words spelled automatically	Refinement of vowel digraphs and long vowel patterns Preconsonant nasals r-controlled vowels Diphthongs wa-, -al Inflectional endings Nonphonetic patterns Large store of known words Handwriting	Multisyllabic words, more awareness of patterns Affixes and roots spelling-meaning connection Refinement of knowledge and use of a variety of strategies More words spelled quickly and correctly	Greater command of an expanding vocabulary Combining forms Changes in consonant and vowel sounds with suffix addition Assimilated prefixes
Strategies	Concept of self as a writer Language development Risk-taking	Sounding out Letter name cues Articulation cues One sound to one symbol relationships	Visualization Letter sequence-sound relationships	Shift from primarily phonetic to other strategies Analogy to known words Meaning-spelling connections Proofreading Syllabication		With unfamiliar words, students often return to a phonetic approach to construct spelling, if other strategies fail Metacognitive awareness

NOTES

VI

Expanding the Spelling Vocabulary: Multisyllabic Words

Before discussing multisyllabic words, let's review the general trends so far. Children initially use their knowledge of letter forms, articulation of sounds, letter names and letter sounds to begin to spell. As well, they begin to learn some spellings by memory which they write easily instead of constructing them each time. They also become aware of letter sequences related to sounds and begin to rely more and more on visual memory of words. If you examine children's writing at this point you will see many phonetic and nonphonetic words spelled correctly. If you have kept samples over time you will notice that incorrectly spelled words are getting closer to standard spelling. If you look at the types of errors rather than viewing the whole word as wrong, you probably can identify what the children know about spelling and what they need to learn.

> Before correcting all the words that are not conventionally spelled, remember to look at the words that are spelled correctly or almost correctly. These indicate what strategies children use to construct spelling and what they know. Compare their present spelling to earlier spelling. Learning to spell takes numerous encounters and experiences with writing and occurs over many years, probably over a writer's lifetime. In fact when can you say one is finished learning to spell? Often it finishes for some children when they become discouraged from overcorrection and unrealistic expectations.

> With incorrectly spelled words, determine if children were using letter name, articulation, phonics, visual or other cues. Sometimes you need to ask the children. (Refer to the list of strategies in Section VIII and the spelling patterns in Tables 7 and 8.)

Although the different spelling patterns are presented in this book one after another, it does not imply this is the only order which children learn them. Often they learn something about different types of patterns concurrently and what they learn facilitates other learning. The process of learning is not linear and clear cut. It is always interactive and depends on whatever children focus their attention on at the moment, what they already know and what they need to learn. Everyone learns something different from a lesson, demonstration, lecture, reading or experience. What is learned is not controlled by what a teacher or other person tries to teach or even by the experience. It depends on what is happening within the learner: a combination of accumulated knowledge, types of experiences, present focus of attention, expectations and goals.

Children's vocabularies continue to expand as they experience life. Thus, they are able to call upon these words to help express themselves in their writing. As children grow and accumulate more knowledge, they become better able to understand concepts, ideas and patterns that they couldn't understand before. To expand their spelling competency, they need to learn the spelling patterns found in multisyllabic words and that these patterns differ from those found in one syllable words.

Learning to spell multisyllabic words involves becoming aware that there are syllables in words. This realization could be compared to their earlier awareness of the

Expanding the Spelling Vocabulary: Multisyllabic Words

concept of word—that there are spaces between words written in sentences.

Some of the patterns related to multisyllabic words are as follows:

Syllables are speech units.

1) A syllable is a speech unit; syllables are thus related to how words are spoken. Have children listen to be aware of each "beat" or part, for example:

- One syllable: *each, fish, did, run, catch*
- Two syllables: *learn· ing, be· come, ex· pand*
- Three syllables: *syl· la· ble, rep· re· sent, un· der· stand*

Every syllable has one vowel sound.

2) Every syllable has one vowel sound (represented by 1 or 2 vowels): **an· i· mal**, *cour· age, cau· li· flow· er.*

Spelling patterns in syllables differ from those in one syllable words.

3) Patterns for spelling sounds in syllables differ from those in one syllable words: *sta· tion* (not **stay·** *tion*), *at· tic* (not *at·* **tick**), *re· main* (not **ree·** *main*), *al· ways* (not **all·** *ways*).

Draft

Note that most of the words are spelled correctly. Less familiar words, *certain* and *allergic*, are constructed using reasonable phonics knowledge and sounding out each syllable: **ser· ten, a· ur· jick**.

Vowel-consonant patterns where syllables join.

4) In identifying syllables, patterns can be seen in the letter sequences where the syllables join, for example, the **vccv** or **vcv** patterns (v = vowel, c = consonant):

  a) Divide between consonants **vc· cv**

  can· dy, sil· ver
  (the middle consonants are different)

  pret· ty, dif· fer
  (the middle consonants are the same)

  b) Divide between first vowel and consonant **v̄· cv**

  ho**· te**l, o**· pe**n
  (the single consonant is placed with the second syllable; in these cases, the vowel sound in the first syllable has its long sound)

  c) Divide between consonant and second vowel **v̆c· v**

  riv· er, **man· a**ge
  (the single consonant is placed with the first syllable; in these cases, the vowel sound in the first syllable has its short sound)

  d) A **consonant** + **le** at the end of a multisyllabic word forms a syllable, for example: cir· **cle**, gig· **gle**, ta· **ble**.

  The vowel sound in the first syllable will help determine whether there will be one or two consonants in the middle:

  short /ă/ sound
  two consonants: *rat· tle can· dle*

  long /ā/ sound
  one consonant: *cra· dle sta· ple*

  Note, this is the same pattern as seen for the above **v· cv** and **vc· v** syllable patterns:

le at the end of multisyllabic words forms a syllable along with previous consonant.

Open and closed syllables.

- When syllables end in a vowel, that vowel has its long sound. This is called an open syllable, for example: **bē·** gin, **ō·** pen, **stā·** ple.

- When syllables end in a consonant, the vowel has its short sound. These syllables are called closed syllables, for example: **rĭv·** er, **măn·** age, **răt·** tle.

Stress or accent on syllables.

5) Usually one syllable is stressed more than the others. In English the stressed syllable is generally the first or second one. This is easily demonstrated by saying people's names that have more than one syllable: **Pe**ter, **Ma**ry, **Em**ily, **Mat**thew, **Su**san. If the second syllable is emphasized, it sounds as if the word is from another language.

Another way to illustrate stress, or accent, is to point out the different stress in words like **rec'·** ord and re· **cord'**, **pres'·** ent and pre· **sent'**. Notice also the shift in vowel sounds following the same pattern of open and closed syllables discussed above.

Children can sort words by these different syllable patterns to discover how spelling works.

Vowels in unstressed syllables have the schwa sound.

6) The spelling of vowel sounds in the unstressed syllables can not always be determined by sounding out. In fact regardless of the vowel used, it tends to have one particular sound, the schwa sound: *composition, narrative, mountain.* These vowel sounds won't have the expected sound. For example, in *syl· la· ble* the **a** does not have its long vowel sound—it has an unstressed schwa sound. This is represented in the dictionary by the symbol / ə /.

Children can learn the spellings of these syllables by focusing visually on the unstressed syllable. Alternatively, they can relate the spelling of these words to their roots or origins or to other words they already can spell. For example, comp**o**sition comes from comp**o**se in which the /ō/ sound is clearly heard.

Prefixes, suffixes and endings are syllables that add meaning to the root word.

7) Prefixes, suffixes and endings are syllables (see Section VII). Therefore, spellings of these and patterns for hyphenation at ends of lines may differ for multisyllabic words. For example, endings, prefixes and suffixes stay together as syllables, hence the hyphen will generally be placed between them and the root words: *fill-ing, land-ed*. However, with multisyllabic words, hyphens are usually placed between middle consonants: *vil-lage, can-dy, sis-ter*. (Note: Consonant digraphs stay together in a syllable: *moth-er, bush-el*.)

In words with only one medial consonant, endings are separate from the root: *com-ing, hop-ing*. The division between the root and ending does not depend on the preceding vowel sound. To maintain the short vowel sound in words with the **cvc** pattern, the final consonant is doubled: *hop, hop-ping*.

This pattern involving endings differs from dividing two syllable words, for example:

- short vowel sound: *riv-er, cam-el* versus *hop-ping*
- long vowel sound: *ho-tel, ti-tle* versus *hop-ing*

These patterns are summarized below. Some of these patterns can be related to the knowledge children have already gained through their experiences in learning to spell other words. For example, some one syllable words illustrate the patterns found in open and closed syllables. For example:

Spelling patterns of vowels in some syllables can be related to similar patterns in one syllable words.

	long vowel sound	short vowel sound
one syllable words	go be	got bed
two syllable words	o· pen be· gin ti· tle sta· ple	bot· tle beg· gar lit· tle can· dy

VII

Beyond Letters Related to Sound: Spelling Relating to Meaning

The underlying regularity of spelling relates letter sequences to both sounds and meaning. To become competent spellers, children must move from reliance on sounds and speech to using visual and meaning relationships as well.

In addition to letter-sound and letter sequence-sound relationships, spelling patterns are related to meaning and word origins. If children continue to use phonics and sounding out as their main strategy for spelling, they will have difficulty remembering the spelling of nonphonetic words. Becoming aware of meaning-spelling relationships provides another useful and necessary strategy for competent spellers.

As mentioned in Section VI about spelling multisyllabic words, the spelling of the vowel sound in an unstressed syllable is often difficult to determine. Frequently though, both spelling and meaning remain related to the word from which it is derived (*describe—description, narrate—narrative*).

Contractions, homonyms and compound words.

The spellings of contractions are directly related to meaning and origin rather than to pronunciation (they're—they are). Homonyms, words that sound alike, indicate different meanings by their different spellings (heir—air). Compound words do not follow the same spelling patterns as multisyllabic words since their meaning is preserved in their spelling (snowflake not snoflake).

Capitals and possessives.

The use of capital letters provides meaning to the written word because it signals to the reader names of people, places, events, books, special things, days, months. Possessives (**'s**) indicate ownership. These are ways that the writing system provides information through spelling to the reader; cues that are not given in speech.

Inflectional endings (ed, ing, s(es), er, est) represent meaning.

Inflectional endings such as **ed, ing, s(es), er, est** also provide meaning to the reader. Although the pronunciation of the ending **ed** has three different sounds (/**ed**/, /**t**/ and /**d**/), it is consistently spelled **ed** and conveys the same meaning. In hyphenation and syllabication, endings form a syllable as a meaning unit. Similarly, the root words to which these endings and suffixes are added generally maintain their spelling. When the spelling changes, it does so following certain patterns such as:

- Dropping the final **e**
  (*make—making*)

- Doubling the final consonant to maintain the short vowel sound before the consonant
  (*stop—stopping*)

- Changing **y** to **i** when adding **ed, er, est** and suffixes that begin with a vowel
  (*carry—carried; envy—enviable*)

- Keeping the **y** when adding **ing**
  (*carrying* not *carriing*)

- Changing the **y** to **i** and adding **es**
  (*carries* not *carrys*)

These and other patterns are described below. When you see them presented all at the same time, it appears that there are so many that it would be impossible to learn them all. If they are presented as lists and as rules, it certainly would be overwhelming, especially if you are not particularly interested in learning about words.

Spelling seems to be a complex skill, but so are speaking, listening, reading, playing music, singing and so on. Children gain competencies in many complex skills by using them.

Learning itself is very complex, yet that is precisely the function of the brain. Children learn how to talk without consciously knowing what they do. They learn to read, draw, act, play, become musicians, artists, mathematicians, writers and so on. If a complete description of all the skills needed for these activities was written down, you would wonder how anyone could learn anything. In reality these activities are learned through experience, just as spelling needs to be learned through actually writing, and reading that writing. Children can learn and figure out these patterns. They may not be able to tell you what they know, but the way they write and what they write is an indication. Children can be helped to learn to spell by others who can point out patterns and spellings. Through understanding and becoming aware of the patterns, children become competent spellers in their writing.

In this section it is easier to present the spelling-meaning connections through examples which highlight the following common patterns:

- Contractions
- Compounds
- Capitals

- Possessives
- Homonyms
- Root Words and Inflectional Endings
- Root Words and Suffixes
- Root Words and Prefixes
- Combining Forms

Contractions

Contractions are two words put together and shortened by omitting a vowel or a consonant + vowel.

Children use contractions in their speaking vocabulary long before they realize that contractions are two words shortened to make one. They understand how to use them in speech very well. However, in their first attempts to spell contractions, children use sounding out strategies and construct such spellings as **didint** or **dident** (*didn't*), **Il** or **Ile** (*I'll*).

When children learn more about language and spelling, they are then able to understand that contractions are related to the spelling of the two words that form them (for example, *they will—theywill—they'll*).

Point out how contractions are formed from two words and how the spelling is related to their meaning. This helps children realize they do not have to memorize each one. If they understand *didn't* means *did not*, then show them that they could think of spelling *didnot* but instead of printing the **o** in not, they put an apostrophe to let people know a letter is missing: *didn't*. See the list of contractions in Table 9.

Table 9 Contractions

is not	isn't	we will	we'll
did not	didn't	you will	you'll
do not	don't	they will	they'll
does not	doesn't	I will	I'll
was not	wasn't	he will	he'll
can not	can't	she will	she'll
could not	couldn't	it will	it'll
would not	wouldn't		
should not	shouldn't	we have	we've
have not	haven't	you have	you've
will not	won't	they have	they've
		I have	I've
we are	we're		
you are	you're	we had (would)	we'd
they are	they're	you had (would)	you'd
I am	I'm	they had (would)	they'd
he is	he's	I had (would)	I'd
she is	she's	he had (would)	he'd
it is	it's	she had (would)	she'd
that is	that's		
		let us	let's

Compound Words

Compound words are made by joining two words together. The spelling-meaning relationship is maintained.

Children use compound words in speaking and listening long before they understand that sometimes two words are put together to form another word. Consequently, they first attempt to sound these words out or spell them as two separate words. Also they have just probably finished realizing that words should be separated by a space. Now they need to know which ones are compounds and shouldn't be separated. They need to learn that in compound words the two words have the same spelling patterns as they have when they are used separately. Thus spelling compound words differs from spelling two syllable words, for example:

compound words	differ from	two syllable words
hillside		fulfil (not *fullfill*)
maybe		maple (not *mayple*)
beehive		begin (not *beegin*)

In many compound words the spelling-meaning relationship is clearly evident (see Table 10).

Capitals

Capitals signal the names of specific things, and beginnings of sentences and speech.

Capital letters provide a signal to the reader that the word is being used to represent names of specific things: people, places, events, titles, days, months and oneself (I). If the place, event, title, and so on is not specific—*prince, island, beach, games* or *aunt*—the word is not capitalized; otherwise it is—*Prince Edward Island, Long Beach, Olympic Games, Aunt Edna*. Capitals are also used to indicate the beginning of a sentence or speech, for example, **T**he child walked away yelling, "**D**on't ever do that again."

Table 10 Some Compound Words

beehive	outside	Sunday	myself
sunrise	baseball	grandmother	ago
maybe	daytime	downtown	bagpipes
around	upset	makeup	anywhere
football	dishrag	birthday	afternoon
everybody	bedtime	raindrop	cannot
inside	everything	inside	birthday
hillside	something	everyone	today
away	airplane	without	anything
mailbox	someone	fireman	cowboy
himself	sunshine	maybe	upon
behind	myself	tonight	grandfather
uphill	along		

The best way for children to learn the conventional use of capitals is by pointing out their use in their reading and writing. Also, children can sort and categorize words according to whether they should be capitalized or not.

In speech, a slight pause is an indication of the end of a sentence. Help children become aware of pauses when they read their own and other writing. By using what they already are familiar with in speech (a brief pause), they can quickly learn where to use capitals (and periods).

Possessives

The possessive form ('s or s') signals ownership.

The possessive form (friend's book) is distinguished from the plural form (my friends) only by the apostrophe used in writing. The 's (or s') is a written signal that ownership or possession is being mentioned. It serves as a visual clue in written language to aid comprehension.

Children must be able to understand this concept. If they have been introduced to the use of punctuation (for example, periods to signal the end of a sentence) and apostrophes in contractions (to signal missing letters), then they will be able to understand that the possessive form is used to add meaning for the reader.

Possession or ownership is shown by adding **'s**:
    uncle's   doctor's   cat's

If the word ends in **s** use just an apostrophe:
    friends'   sisters'   James'   the Jones'

(for names sometimes you might see *James's* or the *Jones's*)

> What make's me mad?
> You know what really make's me made?
> My three brother that's what!
> They are real bugs.
> When I have friend's oevr they won't leave us alone.
> But if I didn't have three brother's there wouldn't be anyone to talk to or play games with.
> So I guess three brother's is not so bad sometime's.

When children become aware of something new, they often use it in all circumstances whether or not it is correct. Sometimes, new learning seems to result in children "forgetting" what was correct. They overgeneralize. Gradually they learn to distinguish the different situations and use it correctly. This 8-year-old is using 's in most words that end in s (*make's, friend's, brother's, sometime's*).

Homonyms

With homonyms, or homophones, different spellings represent different meanings, but the same sound.

Homonyms, or homophones, are words with different meanings and different spellings but the same pronunciation, for example, *there, their, they're; rain, reign, rein; made, maid.* If you begin to focus on finding homonyms in English, you may be surprised to find how many there are. Usually you are not aware of their frequency because they impart meaning at the same time as they are written or read, thus related homonyms do not come readily to mind (see Appendix B).

> Homonyms are often the basis of jokes. Children enjoy learning jokes and making up their own joke books. They can learn to spell these words as they use them in their writing. Many children's books use homonyms to create funny stories. Reading or providing these books for children to read and enjoy helps them realize the fun they can have with language.

Root Words and Inflectional Endings

The spelling of an inflectional ending does not change and reflects consistency in meaning. Minor spelling changes may occur in the root word.

When spelling words with endings (**ing, ed, s(es), er, est**), children first use the strategy of sounding the endings out. They have not yet realized that spelling parts of words may sometimes be related to meaning rather than to sound. The ending **ed** is at first spelled as it sounds: land**id** (*landed*), hop**t** (*hopped*) or plan**d** (*planned*). Beginning writers add these endings to words without awareness of the patterns such as:

- Doubling the final consonant in words with a consonant-vowel-consonant pattern (*rubbed, planner*)

- Dropping the final **e** before adding **ing** in others (*hope, hoping*)
- No change when adding the ending to other roots (*standing, played*)
- Changing **y** to **i** and adding **ed, es, er** or **est**

Children will initially tend to double all final letters or not double any, or seem to indiscriminately double or drop letters. It takes a long time for them to figure out the patterns and apply them consistently. Table 11 on page 88 shows the patterns for adding these endings.

> The meaning of these endings should be pointed out and related to their spelling. This meaning is already understood from speaking and listening. Now their attention needs to be drawn to the spelling-meaning relationship and conventions for adding these endings to words.
>
> Meaning of the endings:
> - **ing**—the action is happening now
> - **ed**—the action has happened already
> - **s (es)**—more than one
> - **er**—more (quantity or quality)
> - **est**—most (quantity or quality)

Words with the ending **ed** can be sorted by their sound and by the types of words to which they are added (finished, painted but not happied, thated). This helps bring awareness to the function and sound of the **ed** ending. Adding **ed** to a word (verb) changes it to mean "in the past" or "already done." Although the ending may have three sounds, it is always spelled **ed**.

- **ed** added to words ending in **d** or **t** sounds like /**ed**/:
  landed, sounded, planted, stunted
- **ed** added to words ending in **k, s, f, p, x, ch, sh** sounds like /**t**/:
  liked, passed, huffed, skipped, mixed, watched, fished
- **ed** added to other words sounds like /**d**/:
  planned, hummed, rubbed, filled

At the same time children may discover words that do not add **ed**. These include words such as sleep, keep, weep (slept, kept, wept) and *write* (*wrote*), *run* (*ran*) and *have* (*had*). Awareness of these spellings is directly related to development of speaking vocabulary. Children gain knowledge of the standard use of these *irregular* words through conversations with others. Children beginning to learn the language say things like "I **runned** all the way" or "I **ranned** all the way" even though they previously used the correct form, **ran**. This is a natural part of learning and indicates that children are actively trying to figure out the structure of the language. In this case, it shows that children realize how to talk about past events. For a while, they seem to confuse the use of *run* and *ran*. Eventually, with

⁜   ⁜   ⁜   ⁜

> This is me bakeing bred yesterday.
> We starsted makeing it without Delay.
> Pots went Flying We were crying
> And Mrs M'wirter was lyein.
> It was so fun I wated to make a bun.
> We set it to rise with a millon Cries.
> when it was cooking there was no looking!
> when it cooked we had a look with a big smile
>   The end.

This 8-year-old adds **ing** to the root words (*bake, make, cry, cook, look*) without changing the root word. As a result the words are correct except for those ending in silent **e**. Note: the child is aware of "changing the **y** to **i** and adding **es**" for *cry—cries*.

Table 11 Patterns for Adding Inflectional Endings

Patterns for adding ed, ing, er and est to single syllable words

Word Pattern (c=consonant v=vowel e=silent **e**)

	cvc	vce	vcc	vvc
Root Word	drop pat	hope trade	jump land	join clean
Pattern	double the consonant	drop the e	no change	no change
ing	dropping patting	hoping trading	jumping landing	joining cleaning
ed	dropped patted	hoped traded	jumped landed	joined cleaned
Root Word	red	fine	fond	clean
er	redder	finer	fonder	cleaner
est	reddest	finest	fondest	cleanest

Patterns for adding ed, ing, er and est to multisyllabic words ending in cvc pattern

	Two Syllables		Three Syllables
	Accent on first syllable	Accent on second syllable	
Root Word	profi<u>t</u>	refe<u>r</u>	benefi<u>t</u>
ed	profited	refe<u>rr</u>ed	benefited
ing	profiting	refe<u>rr</u>ing	benefiting

for some words, doubling the final consonant is optional, for example,
    focus: focussing or focusing
    label: labelling or labeling
    cancel: cancelled or canceled

Table 11 Continued

Patterns for adding ed, ing, er and est to words ending in y

Ending	ing	er
Root Word	carry	happy
ing	carrying	-
ed	carried	-
er	carrier	happier
est	-	happiest

Patterns for Adding s (es)

Root word ends with		Examples
s x ch sh ss	Add es	mix—mixes glass—glasses
y	change y to i and add **es**	worry—worries
ey ay oy	Add s	monkey—monkeys day—days toy—toys
f	sometimes change f to v and add es sometimes no change (pronunciation provides the key)	loaf—loaves thief—thieves roof—roofs chief—chiefs
other words	Add s	jump—jumps picture—pictures

Some words do not change in their plural form: one fish—two fish

Some words change spelling in their plural form: one mouse—two mice

Oral language experience provides knowledge of which words change spelling or remain the same

To help children with spelling these words, realize that:
- Children do not need to memorize the rules. Talking about patterns and sorting words helps them realize patterns and provides them with a way to remember spellings. By sorting verbs in the past tense, note that some end in **ied**. Children can be led to discover these come from root words ending with a **y** (but not **ey** or **ay**).
- Children just beginning to use mainly letter names and articulation cues to construct spelling probably are not ready to look for such patterns. Learning a rule will not make much sense to them. However, after many experiences with actual words and using them in their writing, children may find that learning rules such as "change the **y** to **i** and add **ed**" might help them reconstruct spellings of unfamiliar words.
- Children can develop understanding of adding **ed** to words by finding words that end in **ed** and sorting them. Help them make generalizations about spelling, sound and meaning.

Sounds like				
/d/	/t/	/ed/	\multicolumn{2}{c}{other}
pla**nn**ed	stu**ff**ed	lan**d**ed	ca**rr**ied	led*
gra**bb**ed	mi**ss**ed	plan**t**ed	hu**rr**ied	bed*
spi**ll**ed	mi**x**ed	wan**t**ed		red*
	tri**pp**ed			
	fi**sh**ed			
	clu**tch**ed			
	ki**ck**ed			

*If children mention these words, point out that these do not have the **ed** added as an ending to another word.

awhile, they seem to confuse the use of *run* and *ran*. Eventually, with continued interaction with other people who use the correct form, children do figure out the correct usage and say, "I ran all the way." Developing standard vocabulary use as a result of everyday experiences and discussions will establish the basis for spelling these words correctly.

Root Words and Suffixes

Suffixes added to the end of root words alter the meaning of the root word. Each suffix has a consistent spelling and meaning.

Suffixes are parts of words that carry meaning. These can be added to the end of a word to modify its meaning. For example, *washable*: **able** added to the root word **wash** means that the object is *able to* be washed; *famous*: **ous** added to **fame** means *full of* fame.

Common suffixes are listed in Table 12. In learning the spelling of words with suffixes, it is important to note how the meaning of the root word changes but is still related. It is also important to show children that the suffix is always spelled the same and alters the meaning in a similar way, no matter what word it is added to.

Table 12 Commonly Used Prefixes and Suffixes

Prefixes		Suffixes	
re	again	**ation, ment**	state of
dis	not, reversal	**ture**	result of
pro	in favour of	**ive**	that which
in	into, not	**ness**	state of being
en, em	in, into, cover	**ic**	dealing with
pre	before	**ous**	full of
ad	to, toward	**able**	can be done
com, co, con	with, together	**less**	without
e, ex	out of, former	**ish**	like
sub	under, beneath	**ly**	in manner of
ab	away from	**ful**	full of
be	make, thoroughly	**er, or, ar**	one who
de	downward, undoing	**age**	state of
un	not, opposite	**ism**	belief in
tri	three	**let**	little
super	above, beyond	**ory, ery**	where it is made
anti	against, opposed	**ward**	in direction of
non	not	**al, ial**	related to
mis	wrongly	**logy**	study of
auto	self	**en**	made of
post	after	**y**	marked by

Explain to children the root word quite often keeps its original spelling and pronunciation. In some cases the spelling and pronunciation may change (but only slightly), for example, *happy—happily*. In other cases the pronunciation may change slightly but the spelling remains the same (*define—definition*). Looking for patterns helps children make sense of spelling and therefore helps them remember spellings. Becoming aware of the patterns also provides them with knowledge they can use to construct spellings of other, less familiar words. Once they have made a reasonable guess at the spelling, they will be able to proofread it themselves or look it up in a dictionary. Other patterns children can become aware of are shown in Table 13.

> Help children to see meaning-spelling relationships between words. Analyze multisyllabic words for prefixes, suffixes, root words and combining forms. It is easier to remember something that makes sense or is related to something already known.

Root Words and Prefixes

Prefixes added to the beginning of root words alter the meaning of the root. Each prefix has a consistent spelling and meaning.

Similar to suffixes, prefixes provide meaning. When added to the beginning of root words, they modify the meaning of that word, for example, *rewrite* means write again; *dislike* means not like.

The spelling of prefixes, like suffixes, remains constant. This occurs no matter which word it is added to, resulting sometimes in doubled letters, for example, *misspell, cooperate, reemphasize*. In the past, some of these words (*cooperate, pretest, nonfiction, preschool*) were spelled with a hyphen between the prefix and root. This is now changing. The hyphen is not used except in cases where the word may be misunderstood or misread without

Table 13 Spelling-Sound Patterns for Adding Suffixes

Words Ending in **e** Drop the **e** if the suffix begins with a vowel	love fame grave	lovable famous gravity
Words Ending in **y** Change **y** to **i** and add the suffix	happy envy	happily enviable
Change in vowel sound, but not vowel	gr**a**ve produ**ce** comp**e**te define loc**a**l	gr**a**vity produ**c**tion comp**e**tition definition loc**a**lity
Change in vowel sound and spelling	pron**ou**nce expl**ai**n	pron**u**nciation expl**a**nation
Change in consonant sound, same consonant	criti**c** attrac**t**	criti**c**ize attrac**t**ion
Change in consonant sound and spelling	conclu**de**	conclu**si**on
Other words—no change	wash dark wonder danger	washable darkness wonderful dangerous

the hyphen (coworker—co-worker, unionized—un-ionized). When the prefix self is used, however, a hyphen is always included (self-confidence, self-evaluate).

Once prefixes and roots are learned, remembering when letters are doubled at the beginnings of words such as *accommodation, assign, illegal, irregular* becomes easier. When you look these up in the dictionary, the origins of the words indicate they are words composed of a prefix and root word. In the first two, the prefix actually is **ad** (meaning *to, toward, near*) and in the second it is **in** (meaning *not*). The prefix has gradually changed its pronunciation and spelling over the years to become *assimilated* into the word, probably because it was easier to pronounce with the changed spelling. Therefore, we have *accommodation* instead of *adcommodation, assign* instead of *adsign, illegal* instead of *inlegal* and *irregular* instead of *inregular*. Table 12 on page 92 presents the common prefixes and their meanings.

✧   ✧   ✧   ✧

> "One day an eagel swepet me from the ocan and took me up over 1000 feet high and droped me down.... down...down SPLASH!!! into a small pool." "A little boy saw me and dug a path into the water for me." "And now because of him I'm still alive   Draft

This 8-year-old proofread his work and underlined the words that he feels need to be checked for spelling.

Eagel, swepet, ocan and *path* are words that are less frequently used and have been sounded out. Perhaps *little, dug, alive* and *droped* are more familiar, but the child is personally still not sure. Note with *dropped* that whether or not to double the **p** is a difficult concept to learn and takes a great deal of experience to master.

Note also the use of quotation marks which indicates the child thinks they should go around each sentence rather than at the beginning and end of the person's speech. This child has also become aware of other writing signals such as eclipses, commas, capitals and exclamation marks (*SPLASH!!!*)

> Home work
> "Do your home work,"
> "No, yes, no, you, no, yes, no."
> Then he got a snack.
> So he went to school.
> "do your work," "No, I dont
> have to, Ha ha ha, go to
> the ofise," "no way,"
> "I'll pick you up," "Okay,
> go a hade," "No I'm not,"
> "Okay,"
>
> Draft

This child has become aware of quotation marks indicating speech and change in speaker. It appears the child thinks " comes at the beginning and , at the end of speech. Now that the child is aware of and is attempting to use quotation marks, editing this sample could involve some discussion about what the child has done correctly and what needs to be changed. The child could be asked to check for use of capitals, since there is an indication that he knows about correct usage. Spelling of unfamiliar words (*office, ahead*) could be discussed and related to other known words and strategies. Note in the third line *"No, "Yes, "No, "You, "No, "Yes,* the use of *you* instead of *yes* is probably a "writing error" (like a "typo") rather than a spelling error. Probably in proofreading, the child would correct this.

⁜   ⁜   ⁜   ⁜

Common Roots and Combining Forms

Greek and Latin combining forms impart the same meaning and have the same spelling whether they occur near the beginning or end of the word.

Some common roots to which prefixes and suffixes are added are listed in Table 14 (in no way an exhaustive list). Also listed are some common combining forms. These refer to parts of words that combine to make new words but, unlike prefixes and suffixes, they can be added to the beginning or end of roots: **photo**graph—tele**photo**, tele**graph**—**grapho**phonics.

Is There Only One Way to Spell a Word?

There are acceptable variations in spelling some words.

Sometimes, people cannot agree on the correct spelling of a word. Even different dictionaries give different spellings. This underscores the fact that spelling is an agreed upon way to represent words on paper. Disagreement can stem from the different representation of words in the British and American dictionaries. Some spellings have grown more acceptable to the British and others more acceptable to Americans. Children can learn there is some disagreement about spelling certain words. Children should realize that language and spellings do change over the course of history. Some of the

Table 14 Common Roots and Combining Forms

meter	measure	flec, flex	bend
mit, miss	send	cred	believe
tel(e)	far	chron(o)	time
duc(t)	to lead	flor	flower
phon	sound	man	hand
scop(e)	view	bio	life
the(o)	god	cent	hundred
scrib, script	write	dict	say
pend	hang	duc(t)	lead
graph, gram	write	morp	form
port	carry, harbour, entrance	ped	foot
		phob	fear
ply	fold	photo	light
sign	sign, mark	spect	look

common differences between British and American spellings focus on the following:

-our/-or: colour/color, behaviour/behavior

-ize/-ise: advertize/advertise

-ce/-se: defence/defense, practice/practise (noun/verb)

For two syllable words ending in a consonant-vowel-consonant (cvc) pattern, there may be alternative spellings. Whether the final consonant is doubled when endings are added, generally go by the following patterns:

1) If the accent is on the first syllable, then final consonant is not doubled: *label, labeled, labeling; focus, focused, focusing*

2) If the accent is on the second syllable, then the final consonant is doubled *omit, ommitted, omitting; recur, recurred, recurring*

3) However, in the dictionary both forms are given for some words, for example, *labeling, labelling; focusing, focussing.*

4) If there are three syllables, usually there is no doubling of the final consonant.

VIII

Spelling Strategies Children Can Learn

If you do not know how to spell a word, what strategies do you use to construct its spelling? You will definitely use whatever knowledge you have about sounds of letters and letter sequences, spellings of similar words, and meaning-spelling relationships. Many misspellings are often based on relying too much on sounding out. Misspelling may also result from incorrect letter-sound relations if enough phonics is not known. However, if sounding out is not used, the misspelling may be based on a hazy visual image or on a lack of knowledge of the spelling-meaning relationship. This may result in spellings that have the right letters, but in the wrong sequence or some letters left out.

Spelling errors reflect the knowledge children have about the spelling system and their effective use of strategies (see Table 15). Errors may result from the following:

- Lack of knowledge
- Incorrect knowledge
- Over reliance on one or two strategies
- Ineffective use of a strategy
- Lack of proofreading
- Writing errors similar to "typos" in typing

Table 15 Words Spelled Using Different Strategies and Knowledge

	house	jumped	life
Initial consonant	h	j	l
Initial and final consonants	hs	jt	lf
Consonants and vowel marker	has	jat	laf
Letter names	-	-	lif
Consonants and vowel sound stretched out	haus	-	luef
Articulation cues	hys	japt	liv
Visual strategy used	hose haus hous	jupd	lief
Sounding out prenasal consonant included	-	jumpt	-
Awareness of letter pattern and sounds,	hous house	jumped	lafe life

Development of spelling skills continues throughout life. How competent children become depends on several factors. One of the most important is self-concept:

1) Do they *feel* they are a good spellers?

2) Do they *see* themselves as someone who can learn to spell?

3) Do they *tell* themselves they can be good spellers?

Spelling Strategies Children Can Learn 101

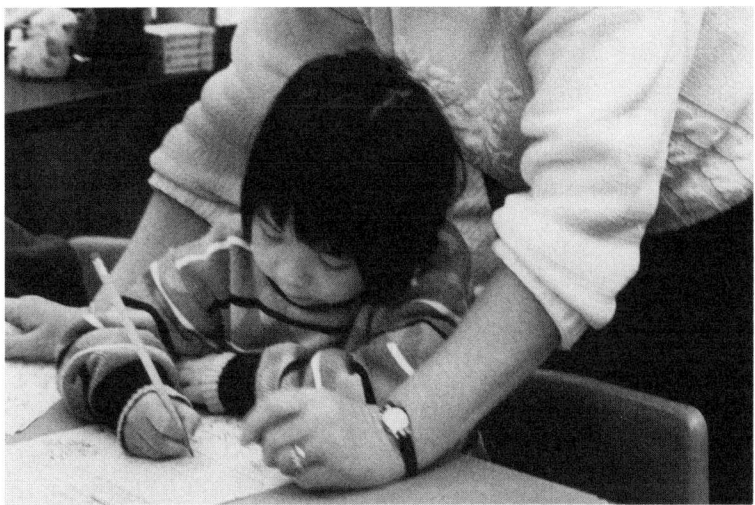

If in the initial experiences with writing and spelling, children are told they can't spell and probably never will be very good, they may end up believing that. This is especially true if they also can't remember the words given in spelling lists or don't enjoy the exercises because they seem to have no purpose or meaning. Factors such as seldom getting A or 100% on weekly tests, or having papers returned with x's, words circled, underlined or corrected, and being told to write out the incorrect words 10 to 20 times discourage children. These do not help children learn to spell or to feel they can be good spellers.

However, if children have developed a positive attitude towards improving spelling, then progress can be made. What helps children keep learning are strategies such as:

- Developing listening, speaking and reading vocabularies

- Being involved in writing activities of interest to them

- Understanding letter-sequence patterns and their sounds
- Understanding relationships between words (define, defined, definition, redefine, etc.)
- Knowing origins of words
- Knowing meanings of word parts
- Realizing that some spellings are unusual and/or unpredictable

In helping children improve their spelling, you need to determine what knowledge or strategies they could learn or use better. The rest of this section describes the strategies children can learn.

A. Develop self-concept or belief that they can spell competently

This may not technically be thought of as a strategy for spelling. However, if children (and ourselves as well) believe they can't spell and will never be able to make sense of such a complicated language, then they will not want to make the effort. The effect of self-concept on learning is well documented. You probably have your own personal experiences that reflect the vital role of self-confidence in motivating learning. It can help you attempt difficult challenges. Difficult usually means that effort is needed to accomplish the task. The effort can be maintained if you feel you will be successful and are confident that you can learn what is necessary to reach the goal.

Children need to view themselves as being able to learn spelling. Without this, trying to help them will be a constant struggle and their lack of desire to learn will be a stumbling block.

Developing a self-concept of being a good speller comes from experiences. It is essential that children experience success and feel they are learning in their beginning attempts to spell. To understand how children learn, you can:

1) Notice what children do know about spelling and relate this to realistic expectations. The beginning speller may not even be able to read. Therefore, they will not know what words should look like. However, by using their knowledge of letters, letter names and articulation cues, children can attempt to write down what they want to say. To expect correct spelling at this point is unrealistic. To correct the spelling is to give children the message they are not spellers. Yet they are doing what all effective learners do and what we as adults do when we don't know how to spell a particular word. They construct the spelling based on what they know.

2) Encourage children to write their ideas and thoughts on paper or use a computer. As they learn more about words through writing and reading, you can gradually point out frequently used words and spelling patterns.

3) Respond to their queries about spelling. For example, if they ask if **HS** is correct for *house*, consider what experience they have had and what they already know. If it is the first time they have tried the word and they are not too sure about themselves as writers, you can simply confirm that they have the right letters for some of the sounds. You will know if you need to go further by the children's responses. Some will be satisfied with that (for now), others will want to know if it is *correct*. In the latter case you can then just show them the correct spelling as "it is written in books," and perhaps relate it to other knowledge they have.

4) When responding to children's writing, comment on the content, on their ideas and thoughts and on what skills they have before pointing out what are generally viewed as "errors." Look at these "errors" as information for how to help children progress. Choose one to two at a time to explain a strategy or expand their knowledge of spelling patterns. In this way children grow in their learning and self-concept.

B. Develop listening, speaking and reading vocabularies

The importance of children being involved in listening, speaking and reading activities has already been mentioned. Through their interactions with others, children listen to and speak the language. This forms the basis of their language knowledge and creates a foundation for writing and spelling. In learning to spell, they use their knowledge about the sounds, words and structures of the language gained through talking and listening. They can attempt to write words they have heard, using the pronunciations they have learned. The source of ideas and thoughts about which they write comes from interactions and sharing experiences. Even without being able to read, children can attempt to write using what they know. Correct spelling, however, cannot be expected until children are able to read those words. Because reading involves recognition of words using other clues beside print, children will be able to read (recognize) more words than they can spell.

> To help children develop spelling skills, a necessary precursor is to expose them to rich speaking, listening and reading vocabularies.

C. Develop interest in words and in finding common spelling patterns

All learning is easier when you are interested. What is the source of this interest? Think of something you really like to learn about and something you don't like to learn about. What is the difference? Some factors might be the following:

- Previous learning experiences, degree of success and feeling of pleasure associated with it

- Existing amount of knowledge or skill on subject or task—this enables you to build on what you already know or can do
- Belief you can learn and that you are good at learning
- Personal satisfaction or benefit from making efforts
- Enjoyment of meeting a challenge and succeeding

Children can develop an interest in words and spelling. Consider that young children enjoy word play such as rhyming, riddles, jokes, word games and puns. If we as adults continue to show our interest, curiosity and enjoyment in these activities, children will see that language and spelling is interesting.

Discovering patterns in spelling also helps make learning spelling easier. Spelling is made more difficult by thinking each word needs to be learned individually and by trying to memorize each word as individual letter sequences. Finding the patterns and relating unfamiliar words to known words reduces the load on memory. Memory is further increased by associating new information with what is already known and finding similarities or differences. The brain works by trying to organize and make sense of new information. When it succeeds, it remembers. We call this process learning.

Remembering something is much easier if the following conditions apply:

- You need to learn it
- You are curious about it
- You can make sense of it
- You use the skill or information frequently

D. Write frequently: the motor patterns and visual images established help with remembering spellings

As mentioned before, memory or learning is enhanced by using a new skill or information. You have many examples in your own life in which you have forgotten things you "learned" because you no longer use that information or skill. With renewed focus on these forgotten areas, you can remember and regain your previous level of competence. However, you need to become actively involved again in order to sustain the achievement.

You do not forget or lose a skill if there has been sufficient understanding and use. So, too, with spelling. Memorizing words from lists, however, does not provide enough use and interest to ensure real learning. Frequent use of words in actual writing activities is the way to ensure children learn and remember spellings. In these activities, printing and writing words helps establish the motor patterns which become engrained, so that words seem to flow from thought to paper without much intentional effort. The visual image from seeing the word helps later in proofreading, that is, determining if it "looks right." This active process of printing or writing words, as one is engaged in meaningful writing, is essential for developing spelling skills. It is important to remember that writing is meaningful for children if it involves their own purposes, needs and enjoyment.

An independent learning strategy involves thinking of the best way to remember the spelling and using that technique. Then it is essential that the words are printed or written rather than simply spelled out loud. By printing or writing the word, motor patterns are established, the visual image is seen again, and the word can be checked or proofread. The final step in spelling is this proofreading. The spelling process is not complete until you have decided the word is spelled correctly.

E. Be willing to construct spellings based on what you know and to choose the one that "looks right"

Too much emphasis in the beginning on correct spelling may inhibit children's willingness to risk writing. It may also stop them from constructing spelling based on what they know. They need to make reasonable attempts to spell unfamiliar words so that there is something to work from. As mentioned before, adults also need to use this strategy in spelling words that

---

Help children focus on the spelling of words by comparing these with words written elsewhere (in lists or in other writing). Although words may be studied individually or in lists, the main focus for using and learning spelling is in frequent writing activities. Children may be helped by concentrating on words removed from the context of their writing, for example, learning 5 to 10 words a week. This procedure should relate to words they use frequently, words they are having problems remembering, or words that exemplify spelling patterns. These words should be familiar to them in their listening, speaking and reading vocabularies. The activities used should be engaging for the children, not a chore.

Teach them an independent study method. Show them how to do the following:

1) Say and look at the word

2) Choose the best strategy that will help them remember the spelling

3) Cover the word

4) Print the word (write word only if handwriting is very easy and readable)

5) Proofread the word, that is, check the spelling carefully

they may have heard and can use in speaking, but have not learned to spell. Many competent spellers write several possible alternatives for unfamiliar words so the one that "looks best" can be used or checked in a dictionary. Even though spell checkers in computer programs provide possible alternatives, the writer must be able to choose the correct one. Also, if the spelling of a word is not a "reasonable guess," the computer spell checker will not be able to provide a correct response.

To effectively construct alternative spellings, children need to become familiar with the other strategies listed here and gain knowledge of the sounds of letters and letter sequences, and spelling-meaning relationships.

F. Use chanting (spelling in rhythms) and knowledge of rhyming words

Some children find that the use of auditory strategies helps. These auditory strategies involve remembering the word by sounding it out, saying parts or syllables, or saying each letter in sequence. To further increase the effectiveness of auditory strategies, the letters should be printed as they are said.

Saying the word in a rhythm sometimes helps. If possible, keep common letter sequences together, for example, *dau ght e r, comm on ly, br ow n, M iss iss ipp i*. Otherwise, create rhythms that seem to come naturally and have children print the word as they say the letters. In this way, they are using several strategies at once. (This could actually be listed as a mnemonic device as discussed later.)

If children are able to easily recall words that rhyme, then this can be another strategy to help generate alternative spellings from which to choose. In other words, this is a way to remember spelling patterns by drawing on what else is known. Thus, if they are wondering how to spell *ball*, they may be able to think of *all, tall, mall* or *wall*. If they can spell one of those words, it will help them construct a good guess for *ball* rather than spelling it **bol** as it sounds. This helps children move from relying totally on letter-sound relationships and sounding out spellings.

G. Use mnemonic devices

Mnemonic simply means memory. Mnemonic devices include any technique that helps you remember something. For example, how can you remember how to spell *mnemonic*? If you know it refers to *memory* and you know that *amnesia* means loss of memory, then being able to hear the **m** and **n** in *amnesia* will help you remember the **mn** in ***mn**emonic*. In this way, you have made sense of the spelling by relating it to something you already knew, thus making it easier to remember. This is why it is important to help children learn about the origins of words and realize that spellings are related also to meaning, not only to sounds.

Another aid would be to mispronounce the word by saying any silent letters or making it sound strange or funny. This also is a way to increase attention to and memory for words like knife (***k** nife*), thumb (*thum **b***), ghost (*g **host***), people (*pe **o** pl **e***).

Making up sentences to relate words with similar spelling patterns is another device. Examples of this technique are: have a s**eat** and **eat** the m**eat**; his d**augh**ter t**augh**t him and he c**augh**t the fish; they went to Ho**ng** Ko**ng** to play pi**ng** po**ng** with Ki**ng** Ko**ng**. If children make up their own sentences, the enjoyment and meaning they bring to the activity will enhance their memory of the spelling.

Making up and learning riddles is something children enjoy. With words they find "difficult" to remember, they can create jokes: What happens in a bakery after midnight when you turn on the radio?—A bun dance (*abundance*). In this way you are also relating the spelling of an unfamiliar word to words already known.

Similarly, looking for little words in bigger words and making sense of them helps the memory process. The princi**pal** is your **pal**. A princip**le** is a ru**le**. An **ant** is a very tiny animal found in a very large eleph**ant**. An *island* **is land**.

The use of acronyms, that is, representing each letter by a word in a sentence, is another way to try to ease the memory load. Children can make up their own, for example *phone* = **p**eople **h**ave **o**ne **n**ew **e**ar.

Mnemonic devices are not the first way to approach the learning of most spellings. However, for those words that may be difficult to remember, creating unusual or novel relationships and increasing meaning in any way possible will help create a lasting impression. Then the spelling will be easier to remember.

H. Learn to visualize words

How can you help children visualize words? Too often the only resource we have is to tell them to look harder and learn them by memorization or to write them out 10 times. However, this does not help them know how to visualize. What does look harder mean? How much is learned from reluctantly copying words 10 times without active attention, for example, putting down a column of c's, then o's, then p's, then y's. Many children do this in their attempt to make this activity more interesting and easier. Writing words out 10 times obviously does not seem to have much purpose to them.

To help children visualize you could do the following:

- Print a word on a piece of paper, a chalkboard or computer screen. Tell them that you are going to erase it but that they will still be able to see it. Most children will understand that they can "pretend" the letters are still there. Then ask them to read the letters once they are erased.

- Print a short word on paper, chalkboard or computer. Tell children that you will pick up the word between your thumb and forefinger and that they will be able to see the word between your fingers. Have them then read the letters that they visualize.

- Ask children to imagine they are watching their favourite T.V. show or playing a computer game. Ask them to watch the screen in their heads to see what is there. Then have them clear the screen and put the letters for a word on the screen. Have them tell you what letters are there.

Whenever they need to learn to spell a word, they can try to visualize the letters in the way that works best for them. Notice that you ask them to "read" the letters rather than spell the word. The use of this word changes the activity from "spelling," which they may not like, to simply reading letters from their screen. Also, children like to be challenged to "read the letters backwards." This is not confusing for them, and provides the motivation to really create a clear image and to maintain it for a few seconds. Children do not have to close their eyes in order to visualize. Both children and adults are visualizing things all the time. It is one way that we recover information from our memories, only we do it so quickly that we are normally not aware of it. (This idea comes from Neurolinguistic Programming. Dilts, R. (1988). The NLP Spelling Strategy. Anchor Point, 2(1), 1-2,5.)

I. Learn how to proofread (not just read)

In learning to read it is important to use context clues along with phonics clues to identify words on the page. Effective readers rely heavily on their background knowledge and what they expect to come next, so that they do not need the complete spellings to read words. As a matter of fact, that is why it is so difficult to proofread both one's own work and that of others. In helping children develop competent spelling skills, you need to help them understand the difference between *reading* and *proofreading*.

In reading, the reader is trying to understand the message of the author and is not concerned about spelling. As a result, often mispellings go unnoticed. It is not that you are not a good reader but that you are using effective reading skills that differ from proofreading. (Did you notice that the word "misspellings" used in the second sentence of this paragraph was incorrect?)

To help those children who are not easily developing good proofreading skills you can:

- Encourage them to go back over their work and underline the words they are unsure of or the ones they know are incorrect. In this way, self-correction is stressed.

- Have them proofread the lines right-to-left, backwards or starting at the end of the writing so the "meaning" of the passage is removed. More attention is focused on spelling than on meaning.

- For some children it helps to hold a ruler or marker under the line they are proofreading.

- Encourage them to put the writing away for a day or so and then proofread it later. Their memory of exactly what they wrote is not so fresh and it then becomes easier to spot errors.

- As with all writers before publishing, have them get another person to proofread their writing.

Strategies Using Knowledge of the Language

J. Use knowledge of letter-sound patterns (see Section IV)

K. Use knowledge of letter sequence-sound patterns (see Section V)

L. Use knowledge about spelling patterns in syllables (see Section VI)

M. Use knowledge about root words and endings, prefixes, suffixes, and combining forms (see Section VII)

N. Use knowledge about the origin of words (see Section VII)

Summary

Competency in spelling is not spelling words correctly 100% of the time, but rather it is related to having a good basic spelling vocabulary including frequently used words, a knowledge of spelling patterns, an ability to construct reasonable spellings and a willingness to proofread or ensure the work is proofread.

In some dictionaries there are at least 600,000 entries. As well, dictionaries do not list all the words there are in the English language. Many scientific and specialized words are not usually included and new words are added all the time to our language. There is no way that any one person will know how to spell all words. Therefore, competency in spelling needs to be defined in terms of being able to express one's thoughts in writing so that the writer and others are able to read the writing. Further competency is gained by being able to easily spell the commonly used words and to construct reasonable spellings for less familiar words. To become more competent, children then need to expand their knowledge of spelling as they learn and read more and their vocabulary increases. Competency increases as they learn to proofread their own work and independently continue to learn about spelling patterns.

Competency in spelling will continue to increase through one's life if one has a self-concept of being a person who can learn to spell and has an understanding of how spelling works.

If you think this seems like too much to learn, remember, children do not need to learn it all at once. Also realize if spelling is used frequently, they do not need to consciously remember individual spellings. Through frequent use, spellings are remembered automatically just as a phone number you use often is remembered without having to sit down and write it out 20 times. Words that are used frequently are remembered not only because they are seen and read so often but also because motor patterns for those common words become established as they are written. This is similar to the touch typist who does not have to look at the keyboard to find letters or the musician who plays musical pieces from memory—the fingers seem to move without thought.

As you observe children writing and spelling and begin to understand more about both the structure of words and your own spelling strategies, you will begin to realize you already know how to help children improve their spelling. You just were not aware of what you knew. In helping children learn to spell, your own spelling will probably improve, just as theirs will if they also help others.

NOTES

IX

Annotated Samples of Children's Writing

Evaluation of spelling and suggestions for helping

This section provides first drafts of children's writing. Because this is a book about spelling the comments will focus on that. However, it is essential that when responding to children's writing, you acknowledge the thoughts and ideas first. The main goal of writing is to develop competency in expressing ideas in written form. (See Appendix A for what else children are learning in becoming authors.)

Before evaluating spelling and other mechanics of writing, ask children to proofread their own work and to underline words they think may be misspelled or that they aren't sure of. During writing, attention is directed to thinking and less to spelling words. The hand may be writing a word, while the brain is thinking ahead. As a result a misspelling may occur just as typing errors occur when the process occurs quickly. An error may be a writing slip rather than a spelling mistake.

In assessing and evaluating children's spelling, the focus will be on what they know and what might be helpful to learn next. It is very difficult to give accurate evaluations based on one sample. Really several samples should be used. Also samples should be taken over a period of time in order to determine if learning is occurring and competency increasing. As well, the written product provides only part of the assessment. The children should be asked about their writing, to explain why they spell words the way they do, if any words could be corrected, and so on.

The purpose of this section then is to demonstrate, given a sample, what might be noted about children's spelling knowledge and strategies. This provides the starting point for knowing how to help them learn more.

Things to notice:

1) Knowledge about:
   - letter forms, articulation, letter names, word concept
   - phonics: letter-sound relationships, letter sequence-sound relationships
   - syllables: spelling patterns and sounds
   - spelling-meaning relationships and word origins
   - sight words: frequently used words, irregularly spelled words

2) Strategies
   - letter forms
   - letter names
   - articulation cues
   - sounding-out/phonics
   - common patterns
   - syllable patterns
   - spelling-meaning relationships
   - visual memory
   - proofreading
   - mnemonic aids

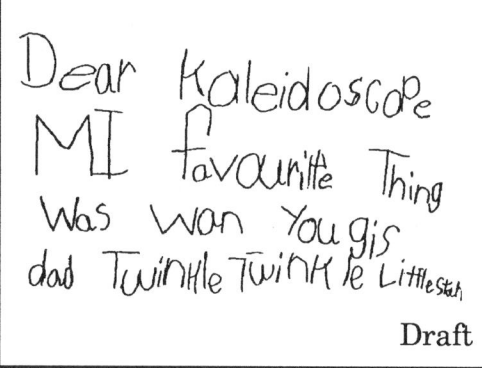

Draft

This child constructs words by:

- using consonant sounds and letter names: **mi** (*my*), **gis** (*guys*)
- using consonant sounds and vowel marker: **wan** (*when*), **dad** (*did*)
- remembering how to spell: *you, was, thing*
- copying words from charts, board or other children: *favourite, twinkle, little, star, dear, kaleidoscope*

Suggestions

This child could begin to learn about different short vowel sounds and the spelling of sight words such as *my* (relate to the pattern: *by, try, fly, cry,* etc.).

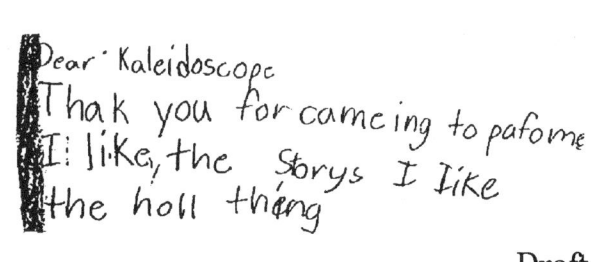

Draft

This child constructs unfamiliar words by sounding out and using visual awareness of word patterns. Note:

- **holl** (aware of **ll** pattern)
- **thak** (omits preconsonant nasal in *thank*)
- **pafome** (reflects pronunciation and awareness of letter-sequence **ome**)

- self-corrected the word *thing*

This child remembers how to spell *like, story, for, to,* and adds endings to known words: story**s**, came**ing** (*coming*).

Suggestions

Continue to develop child's visual approach. Need more samples to determine exactly what to teach.

> Dear Kaleidoscope
> Thank you for showing us the there stories
> I really like them. I like the fisherman one the best I like the part one dawn plaed the flut!
>
> Draft

Many words are spelled correctly indicating good visual memory—note visual strategy attempted for there (three).
- awareness of **ed** ending: pla**ed** (*played*)
- unfamiliar words are sounded out using phonics and letter names: **plaed, flut**

Suggestions

Continue to develop spelling through exposure to language activities and pointing out patterns.

> Dear, Kaleidoscope,
> thank you for showing us us tow Storys.
> i liket your Show.
> it was fun.
> i liket your Songs.
>
> Draft

Many words spelled correctly indicating good visual memory.
- **tow** (*two*) indicates attempt to visually remember spelling

Phonics: sounds out ending **ed** and spells it as it sounds /t/ (**liket**)

Suggestions

Perhaps could begin to learn about adding endings (**ed, s, ing**) to words.

Note: child is aware of periods and commas.

Visual approach indicated by many correct spellings. The child has made some self-corrections and is aware of periods and commas.

Indicates good phonics knowledge:

- knows short vowels and consonant sounds, uses letter sequence-sound patterns and letter names
- **beckam**: maybe hears letter name **k**, but knows there is a **c** in the word, or is aware of the **ck** pattern in words
- **alsow**: aware of **ow** for /o/ sound
- **relly**: uses letter name for /e/ sound and **ll** pattern (*bell, wall*)
- **songhs**: aware of **gh** pattern in words

> Dear Kaleidoscope,
> Thank you for showing us all the the storys my favourit story was How the the Raccoon got his mask. it was relly funny. I liked it best wen the men beckam old and wen the Raccoon played the tricks on the men. I alsow liked the songhs.

Draft

Suggestions

Could learn about **ea** and **ee** pattern. Continue to develop spelling through language activities.

```
onts  Aie   wanT    To
The    bech   and  Aie
       a
 toOnd
 clam   shal    Aie  also
 foond  som    crabs
 andr   rooks   Aie
 so    a   brid   To
 Aie   also   so
 fash   Aie  so   a   a
                     famly  of
```
Draft

Written by an 8-year-old.
Once aie (I?) went to the beach and I found a clam shell. I also found some crabs under rocks. I saw a bird too. I also saw fish. I saw a family of shrimp.

Note the vocabulary used is mainly one-syllable words.

Relies on phonics and sounding out:

- knows consonants, and consonant digraphs and blends: **bech, shal, fash, crabs**
- includes prenasal consonants: **shramp, want, faond**
- tends to use **a** to mark vowel placement: **sam** (*some*), **want** (*went*), **fash** (*fish*)
- uses letter name: **bech** (*beach*)
- knows sound of /ŏ/: uses it for **so** (*saw*)

Some use of visual strategy:

- knows *to, the, and, also, of.*
- puts **brid**, instead of **bird** (very common misspelling in children's early writing)
- aware of **ly** sound and spelling (fami**ly**)
- spelling of **fa**o**nd** (*found*) and **roo**ks (*rocks*) indicate visual approach, knows there should be 2 letters in the middle of the words
- **onts** (*once*): combination of visual and phonics strategies

Suggestions

This child could focus on learning:

- short vowel sounds
- long vowel and **ll, ck** patterns
- **en** has sound of letter name **n**
- visual strategies to remember sight words such as *saw, once, some*

> **Draft**
> joggol I woe trachal it wos vareykawid in The
> pay Gnaly I soa Bisee saging my
> Tok He got a wed Thing Iw tort to see wot it woe
> it wos Hot I ran bak He brt The Tree I jut up And
> Hit Him He folban too osr pepl rad Him And ran
> away wiThe Him I wat awt I woe lianingn
> to The Booafl sown of The joggol The sas of

Written by an 8-year-old.
It was very crowded in the jungle. I was a tarantula. I was busy chasing my prey. Suddenly I saw a scientist. He saw me. He shot a harpoon. He missed. I ran into a tree trunk. He got a red thing. I waited to see what it was. It was hot. I ran back. He burned the tree. I jumped up and hit him. He fell down. Two other people grabbed him and ran away with him. I went out. I was listening to the beautiful sound of the jungle. The sounds of...

By using constructed spellings which are readable, this child is able to develop his writing skills as his spelling improves. If perfect spelling was required, very little would get written. It is important to encourage children to write even if their spelling is not standard. This child's vocabulary extends beyond one syllable words.

Relies on sounding out and phonics:

- aware that spelling of a word should be same each time: **joggol** (*jungle*), **wos** (*was*), **soa** (*saw*), used consistently

- knows consonants and short vowel sounds, aware of **ee** (tr**ee**), **ay** (p**ay** (*prey*), aw**ay**), **oo** (harp**oo**n)
- sounding out poses difficulties with multisyllabic words **trachal** (*tarantul*), **siats** (*scientists*), **lianingn** (*listening*), **booafl** (*beautiful*)
- omits preconsonant nasals: **jut** (*jumped*), **wat** (*went*), **tak** (*trunk*)
- perhaps some pronunciation (speech) difficulties, **wed** (*red*), **osr** (*other*), **kawid** (*crowded*)
- also uses letter names, **vare** (*very*), **pepl** (*people*)

Correctly spelled words: *I, me, hot, tree, ran, the, in, my, got, thing, into, he, up, hit, him*

Suggestions

This child could begin to focus on:

- phonics-sounding out strategy: review digraphs (**ch, sh, th**) consonant blends (**tr, pr,** etc.), preconsonant nasals (**m, n**)
- developing visual memory strategies for frequently used words (*was, other, people, went, busy*)
- **ed** ending and its meaning and various sounds

124   A Guide to Children's Spelling Development

> wons apon a time ther wos a moce namde jac he climd up the tree wen he got to the top ther wus a scwrll, he uwt smrtede hem the mucee didint kick that he gav hem the old one two three in the belee then the moce ran for hes luef then coogr cam to sav hem But the coogr just wontid him for his supr. he at him for his supr.
>
> Draft

Written by a 7-year-old.
Once upon a time there was a monkey named Jack. He climbed up the tree. When he got to the top, there was a squirrel. He out smarted him. The monkey didn't like that. He gave him the old one-two-three in the belly. Then the monkey ran for his life. Then a cougar came to save him, but the cougar just wanted him for his supper. He ate him for his supper.

Visual strategies:
- knows many common words: *time, he, up, the, tree, that, to, the, one, two, three, for, then*, etc.
- beginning awareness of patterns, **ed, oo, time**

Phonics:
- knows short vowel sounds, consonants, blends, digraphs

- relies mainly on sounding out 1 letter for 1 sound, **supr** (*super*), **scwrll** (*squirrel*), **wontid** (*wanted*), **wons** (*once*), **didint** (*didn't*)
- sometimes stretches vowel sounds out too much: **luef** (*life*), **uwt** (*out*)
- words not consistently spelled, **moce, mucee** (*monkey*), **wos, wus** (*was*), **hem, him** (*him*), suggests this child is constructing these words each time, unaware that he has spelled them before

Suggestions
- because he shows awareness of letter patterns such as **oo** (c**oo**gar), **ee** (tr**ee**), **ck** (li**ck**), **i_e** (t**i**m**e**), he is probably ready to focus on other letter sequence-sound patterns such as, **er** (supp**er**), **ou** (**ou**t), **ar** (sm**ar**ted), **ck/ke** (li**ck**/li**ke**), **qu** (**qu**irrel), long vowel with **e** marker (came, gave, ate)
- also focus on more sight words and visualization strategies (*was, there, once*)
- could begin to discuss meaning-spelling relationships, such as **ed** ending and contractions

> One cool morning the sqirel famly was geting rety for winter Mother sqirel and Fother sqirel toild ther babys abowt danger in thie mornig the werst danger of oll come the Bolldegil the egil olmost took the babys when it was nihgt time Mother sqriel looked up at a tree and thot it was a gint bot it was wet and ruff weth finggers and he hred smqing she was scerd
>
> Draft

Written by an 8-year-old.
One cool morning the squirrel family was getting ready for winter. Mother squirrel and Father squirrel told their babies about danger in the morning. The worst danger of all came, the bald eagle. The eagle almost took the babies. When it was night time, Mother squirrel looked up at a tree and thought it was a giant, but it was wet and rough with fingers and he heard singing. She was scared.

Evidence of using sight words (*one, mother, baby, took, was,* etc.), visual memory (*nihgt, finggers, tolld, sqirel*) and sounding out using phonics (*sqirel, olmost, thot, gint, bot, ruff, weth, Fother*).

- generally, the short vowels are used correctly, as are most long vowel patterns
- aware of **ed, ing, s** (for plurals)
- using an effective variety of strategies
- the different spellings of *morning* is probably a writing error rather than a spelling error

Suggestions

- ready to learn more about letter sequence patterns: **wor** (we**rs**t—**wor**st), **ou/ow** (ab**ou**t), **qu** (**squ**irrel), **al** sounds like **ol** (**al**l, b**al**d)
- learn sight words: *there, thought, father, ready, etc.*
- discuss adding endings: baby—bab**ies**, get—get**ting**

> One warm afternoon their was a raccoon his name was Fred. Fred lived In a tree Fred lived In a tree that looked gray. And he nu that a anary lived In the gray tree. Then the raccoon heard a nowes 1 It sawned like a grasshopper he hered that nowes agan It was a grasshopper bot he never So It. He was schared so he went to slep. The nexst morning Fred went gostars to eat his brexchfist when Fred was haf wha up the stars he sliped and he laned on the bulom of the stars weth a big plop Finly Fred got up to the top of the stars and he nu the grasshopper was plaing tricks on him Then Fred hered bark falling from the tree. Fred went for a afternoon nape. wen he was aslip he heared a big crack It whock him up and he looked out the wendo he so...

Draft

Written by a 7-year-old. One warm afternoon there was a raccoon. His name was Fred. Fred lived in a tree. Fred lived in a tree that looked gray. And he knew that an enemy lived in the gray tree. Then the raccoon heard a noise. It sounded like a grasshopper. He heard that noise again. It was a grasshopper, but he never saw it. He was scared so he went to sleep. The next morning, Fred went upstairs to eat his breakfast. When Fred was half way up the stairs, he slipped and he landed on the bottom of the stairs with a big plop. Finally, Fred got up to the top of the stairs and he knew the grasshopper was playing tricks on him. Then Fred heard bark falling from the tree. Fred went for an afternoon nap. When he was asleep he heard a big crack. It woke him up and he looked out the window. He saw...

This 7-year-old has developed effective phonics and sight word spelling skills.

Visual strategies:

- spells many words correctly: *was, name, afternoon, warm, raccoon, looked, lived, then*

Phonics strategies:

- aware of letter sequence-sound correspondences
- unfamiliar words are constructed using phonics: **anamy** (*enemy*), **brexchfist** (*breakfast*)
- **scharid** for *scared* may result from stretching sounds out too much so **h** is inserted

- **nowes** (*noise*) may indicate attempt to visually recall the word using **ow** instead of **oi** and putting **e** before the **s**; or sounding out /oi/ may result in hearing the letter **o**, followed by feeling the mouth take the same shape as it does to say the sound /w/
- **sawned** (*sound*), may have learned **aw** instead of **ow** for /ou/ sound; or sounding word out hears the /a/ and /w/ sounds
- over generalizes the **ed** ending that sounds like /d/: saw**ed** (sound), hear**ed**, her**ed** (heard)

- still uses letter name strategy sometimes: sl**e**p (sl**ee**p), upst**a**rs (upst**ai**rs), n**u** (n**ew**), wend**o** (wind**ow**)

Suggestions
- develop a balance of visual and phonics strategies
- review long-vowel patterns: **ee, ea, oa, ai, o_e, a_e,** etc.
- focus on vowel diphthongs: **ou, ow, oi, oy, oo, ew,** etc.
- teach proofreading strategies
- point out patterns that sound like their letter names: **ef, el, en, em, es, ex**.
- continue to develop sight words and visualization: *half, saw, heard*

Draft

Written by a grade 2 student.
I was flying along I saw some birds and they tried to knock me down but they didn't knock me down and I kept on going to my nest (it) was gone to another tree. That tree was getting chopped down but the Father took the babies to the next tree and the mother found the nest and the Father took the babies for lots of rides and then the Father was so tired. Then the Mother started to fly.
The end

Many sight and phonetically regular words are spelled correctly.

- adds **ing** correctly: *flying, getting*
- perhaps relies more on visual strategies than phonics, but uses both effectively

Suggestions
- focus on developing more phonics knowledge that can be used for constructing unfamiliar words such as *kept, chopped, took, found, start*
- review sounds of **c**—sounds like /**k**/ before **a, o, u** and like /**s**/ before **i, e, y**
- teach **oo, ou, oi, ew, ar**
- discuss contractions: *couldn't, didn't*
- continue to develop sight words

> One day mother squirrel went to go and get some nuts in the old oak tree me and sister squirrel were palying a game called cach the nutll. We looked way up at the giant aak tree that looked like a piece of wood with long arms and fingers sticking out Our noses brushed agamst hard wrinkly bark. It felt rugged. soon mother squirrel came back. mother tucked me and sister squirrel to bed in the morning I heared the birds chirping. I went to go and see wut was the mater. the mother bird said that the grayt big bird wich was a bald eagle stowl one of her baby birds. I went to go and wock up my mom and dad and my sister my dad said wut is the mater. I said we haft to to help our next dornaders. why said fother. because one of her babys is in grate danger. we went to Mount everist to find the bird
>
> Draft

One day mother squirrel went to go and get some nuts in the old oak tree. Me and sister squirrel were playing a game called catch the nut. We looked way up at the [giant oak tree that looked like a piece of wood with long arms and fingers sticking out. Our noses brushed against hard wrinkly bark. It felt rugged. Soon (this section was written by the teacher)] mother squirrel came back. Mother tucked me and sister squirrel to bed. In the morning I heard the birds chirping. I went to go and see what was the matter. The mother bird said that the great big bird, which was a bald eagle, stole one of her baby birds. I went to go and wake up my mom and dad and my sister. My dad said, "What is the matter?" I said, "We have to help our next door neighbours." "Why?" said father. "Because one of her babies is in great danger." We went to Mount Everest to find the bird.

This child's writing reflects effective use of variety of strategies. Knows many words from memory.

Unfamiliar words are constructed using phonics and visual strategies:

- **palying**: may be writing error
- **heared**: apply generalization of adding **ed** to *hear*
- **wut, wich, cach, mater**: sounded out, therefore missing silent letter
- **stowl, grate, grayt**: using knowledge of letter sequence-sound relationships—does not visually recognize correct spelling
- **haft, fother, everist:** as they sound when spoken
- **wock**: shows confusion with **woke** pattern
- **dornaders** (*door neighbours*): sounded out as if one word; reversal of

b is not a problem as it is the only time it occurs; indicates attention was on figuring out spelling rather than printing

Note the use of apostrophes: *wen't, bird's, baby's*. The child has become aware of possessives and contractions. It is typical for children to over generalize something they have just learned and therefore apply it incorrectly. Gradually with use and feedback, they learn when and where not to use apostrophes.

Suggestions

- focus on learning more of the frequently used sight words and use visualization strategies (*great, catch, which, half, what, father*)
- have child learn to proofread spellings
- discuss the use of apostrophes

Draft

I am a diver. I go down deep. I'll tell you about one of my adventures. Well, I went down 53 ft. I was walking on the bottom. I had a spear gun. A shark. It was dramatic. I had to get my spear gun out. I fill(?) shot it. I was walking another mile then I jump and I land on a stingray. I jump again. I drew my spear gun. I killed it. I went to the surface and I went home. The end.

Visual Strategies:

- knows many sight words, for example, *walk, was, down, jump, went, one*
- most one-syllable words spelled correctly, some errors due to focus being on writing ideas down, for example *my* spelled *me* the first time and *my* the second time; check to see what the child can self-correct

Constructed spellings indicate good understanding of phonics and letter sequence patterns:

- awareness of letter sequence-sound relationships: **depe** (*deep*)
- visual appearance: **aubot** (*about*), **botom** (*bottom*)
- less familiar words, **aventres, sper gun, dr madik, srfis, cild**, indicate student is sounding out words and relating own pronunciation to knowledge of phonics—indicates ability to break words into syllables

Suggestions

- point out some patterns for spelling syllables: **ture** (adven**ture**), **ic** (dra-ma**tic**) patterns—discuss using more visual approach to spelling syllables
- review sounds of **c**—sounds like /**k**/ before **a, o, u** and like /**s**/ before **i, e, y**
- review long **e** patterns **ee, ea, e_e** (d**ee**p, sp**ear**)
- review **r** influenced vowels **ar** (sh**ark**), **er, ir, ur** (s**ur**face)

Draft

Written by a grade 3 student.
One day two kids went to an island and they got lost and they did not know where to go. One boy had a knife. The other had the same and just then we heard a noise and then (?) some thing happened. Chap. 2 A tiger jumped out of the bush. He tore the knife and threw it at his prey. The tiger skin kept them warm for a week. Then they went to a side of the island and walked and walked and walked (the) about 2 miles. They found the boat. The End.

Would want to know what words the student could correct or identify as being incorrect, for example, is **wend** (*went*) or **tow** (*two*) a writing error, a pronunciation error or a visual memory error?

Visual strategy indicated by attempted spellings of irregular words: **wack** (*walk*), **were** (*where*), **when** (*went*), **throu** (*through*, although child really needed to use threw), **happind** (*happened*), **tow** (*two*), **milses** (*miles*), **nigh** (*knife*, the student probably knows knife has silent letters and is aware of **igh** pattern for long **i** and /**f**/ sound of **gh** as in *laugh*).

- does have some basic sight words, *one, tiger, about, they, other*

Knowledge of phonics:

- aware of letter sequence patterns **ou, ay, oy** (*noys*), **igh, ed, bote** (*boat*), but does not recognize when word is incorrectly spelled

- check knowledge of short /ŭ/ sound: **jomt** (j**u**mped), **jost** (j**u**st), **bosh** (b**u**sh)
- most words are one syllable words

Suggestions
- continue to refine visual strategies, since indication is that student is trying to use them, but not effectively, (*know, where, through, walk, knife*)
- assess reading ability—can the child read these words?
- assess short vowel sounds to determine what needs to be taught
- review **oy-oi** pattern, long vowel patterns
- review sounds of /**ed**/ as in **jompt** (*jumped*)

> The grate Sea
>
> One sunny day I went skverdiving. I saw an eletrech ell and it thot I was going to kell it with my spergun so it wint away. a stingray it trde to sting me but I sot it weth my spergun. I met Jonthen I asked him how his lag. was doing He saed it was good.
>
> Draft

Written by a grade 3 student.
The Great Sea Adventure. One sunny day I went scuba diving. I saw an electric eel and it thought I was going to kill it with my spear gun. So it went away. A stingray (it) tried to sting me but I shot it with my spear gun. I met Jonathan. I asked him how his leg was doing. He said it was good.

Writing errors probably account for some spelling errors, **weth** (*with*), **sot** (*shot*), **wint** (*went*), **kell** (*kill*). Have the student proofread and correct as many words as possible first.

Visual strategies:
- most sight words spelled correctly. Check other writing to see if *said* is spelled **saed** consistently. Knows there are 2 vowels in this word

Phonics knowledge:
- used for constructing unfamiliar words, **skverdiving** (*scuba diving*), **eletrech** (*electric*), **spergun** (*spear gun*), **thot** (*thought*), indicates reasonable attempts to use phonics based on his pronunciation of words
- aware of long vowel patterns, **tride** (*tried*), perhaps relates word to spelling of rhyming words (*ride, side*); aware of vowel-consonant-silent **e** (**grate**) pattern

- uses letter name strategies to help construct unfamiliar words, **lag** (**leg**), **spergun** (**spear gun**)

Suggestions
- assess knowledge of short /ĕ/ and long /ē/ sounds
- continue to encourage visual strategies
- continue to expand sight word base
- assess other writing samples
- expand skills into spelling multisyllabic words

Draft

Written by a grade 3 student
One day in Eastern Canada some pilot whales beached themselves and some people found them and called the SPCA and they called the fisheries people. The fisheries people came in with a front end loader and a dump truck. Then they picked up the whales but they found out that they had no room in the aquarium.

So they took them to Sea Land in Victoria, B.C. Then they kept them there for two months and they set them free in Bonavista harbor. The End. A note from the author. It is all the pollution that we are dumping into the water that's affecting the whales brains that's why they're beaching themselves.

Find out what the student can correct. Did the student use charts, a book or other people to help with spelling some words (e.g. *pilot whale*)?

Visual strategy:
- has basic sight words: *front, why, they, their, there, whales, some, found*

- attempting visual strategy: *pepole, tow, anather, braens*

Phonics patterns:
- confuses **ck–ke** pattern: **piked** (*picked*)
- aware of letter sequence-sound relationship: **ea** (b**ea**ched, **ea**stern), **a_e** (wh**a**l**e**), **ou** (f**ou**nd), **oo** (t**oo**k), **oo** (r**oo**m), **ee** (fr**ee**), **ll** (uses it to construct **sellvs** (*selves*))

Multisyllabic words reasonably constructed using phonics (divides words into syllables as pronounced):
- **acwereeam** (*aquarium*) (check knowledge of **qu**)
- **fishries** (knowledge of **ies** pattern)
- **pollushin** (can become aware of **tion**)

Suggestions
- check knowledge of **ai** pattern: br**ae**n (brain)
- review **ck-ke** pattern
- review sounds of **c**: **ci, ce, cy** have /s/ sound; **ca, co, cu** have /k/ sound
- continue to learn sight words
- teach syllable patterns such as **tion**

> On a nice day, I was loking out my window and I said to my Mom I will de at the beach. OK, my Mom said.
> So I went out side you pleas get me a plastck oh bag. Mom can thank "you."
> Now, wate will I get.
> A clame, a Ouistr, a rook, a sea shal, a snal, sume barnaculs, a sand crad, and some sea weed.
>
> Chaptr 2, Going home
>
> I hade a good day. Hi Mom. hi how at the beach? ded you do good, I found a clame, a ouistr, a rook, a Sea Shal, a snal Sume barnaculs, a Sand crab and Sume Sea weed.

Draft

Written by a grade 3 student.
On a nice day, I was looking out my window and I said to my mom. "I will be at the beach." "OK," my mom said. So I went outside. "Oh mom, can you please get me a plastic bag?" "Thank you." Now what will I get. A clam, an oyster, a rock, a sea shell, a snail, some barnacles, a sand crab and some sea weed.
Chapter 2, Going Home.
I had a good day. "Hi, Mom." "Hi, how did you do at the beach?" "Good, I found a clam, a oyster, a rock, a sea shell, a snail some barnacles, a sand crab and some sea weed."

Have the student proofread work. Some words are spelled both correctly and incorrectly. Reversals, **de** (*be*), **crad** (*crab*), are probably writing errors—uses **b** and **d** appropriately in all other words.

Uses both visual strategies and knowledge:

- has a basic sight vocabulary, *nice, day, looking, was, out, my, window, beach, said, will* and so on
- aware of letter sequence patterns **ea, ou, ee, oo**
- aware of **e** marker, but not used correctly, **hade** (*had*), **clame** (*clam*)

Constructs words using phonics knowledge: **barnaculs** (*barnacles*), **ouistr** (*oyster*), **plastck** (*plastic*), but doesn't seem to know about **le, oi, ic** patterns.

Suggestions

- check knowledge of **ck** (**rook**-*rock*), **ai** (**snal**-*snail*), **ell** (**shal**-*shell*) patterns
- encourage self-corrections and proofreading strategy
- continue development of sight words: *what, please, some* (if not writing errors)
- review role of silent **e** marker
- review patterns such as **el** which has the sound of /l/; **ll, ck, ai** and **oi** patterns
- point out spelling of syllable patterns **ic, le**

> One day me and my sister wher on the bhech. and then we wher in a little bout. and then we saw a very little iLand. So we whent to it and we saw some sharks arond the iLand and then we Jumpd over the sharks and then we swam back home and then we neve went to the beach agen
>
> Draft

Written by a grade 3 student.
One day me and my sister were on the beach and then we were in a little boat and then we saw a very little island. So we went to it and we saw some sharks around the island and then we jumped over the sharks and then we swam back home and then we never went to the beach again.

whent (*went*, spelled correctly in the last sentence), **bhech** (*beach*) and **neve** (*never*) may be writing errors.

Visual strategies:

- has some sight words, *some, little, very, saw*
- confuses some patterns, **bout** (*boat*), **wher** (*were*)

Phonics:

- aware of letter-sequence patterns, consonant digraphs, vowel digraphs, diphthongs, **ar** and **ck** patterns
- **iland** (*island*) is not a frequently used word so it is constructed based on pronunciation and phonics

Suggestions

- have student proofread, self-correct errors or underline words she is not sure of
- continue to develop sight words (*were, again*) and focus on words that are being confused, **wher** (*were*), **bout** (*boat*), **arond** (*around*)
- discuss **ed** ending, **jumpd** (*jumped*)
- review vowel patterns such as **ou, ow**

> One day I was sitting on the shore
> when I saw a baby dollfin beached.
> I ran over to it, the mouther
> was getting to close so I hade to
> skar her away. I stared to push
> the baby out to sea it touck m
> a wall but I got her friee.
> I sat back on the rooks the baby
> cald and it soond like thank you.
>
> Draft

Written by a grade 4 student.
One day I was sitting on the shore when I saw a baby dolphin beached. I ran over to it. The mother was getting too close so I had to scare her away. I started to push the baby out to sea. It took me awhile but I got him free. I sat back on the rocks. The baby called and it sounded like thank you.

Note the handwriting error: uses **v** for **u**.

Probably **rat** (*sat*) and **stared** (*started*) are writing rather than spelling errors

Uses phonics knowledge and sounding out, but not as effectively as possible.

- constructed spellings show awareness of letter-sequence patterns, **skair** (*scare*), and of using other analogies to other words, **shour** (*shore*—**your**), **dallfin** (*dolfin*—**ball**)
- check knowledge of **ook**/ock (**touck/rooks**), ran/rain

Has awareness of inflectional endings: sett**ing**, get**ing**, ca**ld** (*called*), star**ed** (*started*), beach**ed**.

- student needs to proofread first in order to determine if she can visually recognize incorrect words and unusual patterns: **friee** (*free*), **touck** (*took*)

Suggestions

- discuss letter formation: **u** and **v**
- after the student proofreads, review patterns such as **oo, ee, ai** and extend phonics knowledge
- extend sight word base: **mouther** (*mother*), **to** (*too*), **hade** (*had*), **rain** (*ran*), **shour** (*shore*), **skair** (*scare*)

Annotated Samples of Children's Writing

> One day Jim woke up and saw a 2000 foot plant. Now Jim being verey cerios desided to climb the plant When he got to the top he sow a big castle and he said "I shere am hungry," he said."I'le ask whoever lives there for breakfist", said Jim. "I shere hope they have cornflakes" he said. When he noked on the door a huge giant opencd the door and said in a deep voice "What do want?!" he belowed. "I whould like some breakfest" said Jim. "Hey arnt you Jack?" asked the giant. "Nope Im Jim" he replied. "Oh well onec a boy named Jack stolle some of our gold hen and a harp" he said ".And Ive been misrible even sence
>
> Draft

Written by a grade 4 student.
One day Jim woke up and saw a 2000 foot plant. Now Jim being very curious decided to climb the plant. When he got to the top he saw a big castle and he said. "I sure am hungry," he said. "I'll ask whoever lives there for breakfast," said Jim. "I sure hope they have cornflakes," he said. When he knocked on the door a huge giant opened the door and said in a deep voice. "What do you want?" he bellowed. "I would like some breakfast," said Jim. "Hey aren't you Jack?" asked the giant. "Nope, I'm Jim," he replied. "Oh well, once a boy named Jack stole some of our gold, hen and a harp," he said. "And I've been miserable ever since."

This is a retelling of a story read to the class by the teacher.

Note the number of correctly spelled words requiring both visual and phonic strategies. Note the range of vocabulary.

- some spelling errors involve words that are not frequently used: **desided** (*decided*), **cerios** (*curious*), **breakfist** (*breakfast*), **belowed** (*bellowed*), **stolle** (*stole*), **misrible** (*miserable*); these are not expected to be correct, but note how close they are

- constructs contractions using both visualization and phonics: **I'le** (*I'll*), **arnt** (*aren't*), **Ive** (*I've*), **I'm** (correct)

- visual strategies also indicated by correct sight words and approximate construction of **onec** (*once*), **stolle** (*stole*—knows ll pattern), **breakfist** (*breakfast*), **whould** (*would*—confuse w-wh pattern)

Suggestions
- have the student proofread and self-correct work
- review error patterns that involve frequently used words (*would, sure, very, since*) and words that may be used again (*curious, decided*)
- could begin to discuss prefixes and suffixes (miser**able**)
- review contractions

Written by a grade 4 student.
Jim woke up one morning and he saw a beanstalk outside his window. Then he started to climb the extremely big beanstalk. When he got up he saw a big giant. Then the giant said, "You are safe. I have no teeth." So Jim went in and Jim said, "Have you ever tried false teeth?" And the giant said, "No." And the giant said, "I will pay you good money for these false teeth you say." So Jim got the money and got him false teeth. Then the giant said, "I have another problem. I can't read my printing." Jim said, "Have you ever tried glasses?" "No," said the giant. "I will give you more good money." So Jim got him glasses. "Now I have one more problem. I used to have nice red hair." Jim said, "Have you ever tried a wig?" "No. I will give you more money." So Jim gave him his wig and the giant said, "Now I can eat." Jim ran down the beanstalk and chopped the beanstalk down and a letter came down that said to Jim, "Thank you for all the stuff. From your friend the giant.".

Written by a grade 4 student, retelling a story read to class by the teacher.

- have the student proofread and self-correct; probably writing errors are **Jam** (*Jim*, only once), **priting** (*printing*), **ent** (*end*) and maybe **sow** (*saw*), **reed** (*read*)
- note most words are conventionally spelled
- to construct unfamiliar words student uses a variety of strategies including phonics and visual memory: **clim, sow, a nuther, cant, reed, choped**, and analogies to other known words: **youst** (*used*), **tride** (*tried*), **theys** (*these*)

Suggestions

- continue encouraging spelling skills through language activities
- some focus could be given to patterns of adding **ed** endings: chop**ed**, tri**de**, youst
- review useful sight words: *saw, climb, another, read, can't, these, used*

Written by a grade 4 student, retelling a story read by the teacher.

- note the range of vocabulary and that most words are spelled correctly
- have the student proofread and self-correct to determine which misspellings may be writing errors, for example, **dont, breakfatast, boke**
- aware of apostrophe in contractions, **can't**, but it is not used in **dont**
- not expected to know, *knocked, answered, climbed*

Suggestions

- continue spelling focus within language activities
- encourage proofreading
- review **ow** for long /o/ sound
- focus on words with silent letters and ways to remember them, *climbed, knocked, answered*

Written by a grade 4 student.
Once upon a time there lived a boy. His name was Jim. One morning Jim saw an enormous plant growing outside of his window. So he climbed it. When he got to the top, he saw a castle. Jim wanted to have breakfast there. When he got there Jim knocked. A big giant answered, "Come in. I don't have any teeth to eat you with." He eat breakfast with the giant. "I can't read any more with my eyes. The print is so small too." "Then why don't you get glasses." "I will give you good gold if you get me glasses." "OK," Jim said and off he went. When Jim came back he had the giant's glasses so he could read. "But I still can't eat anything I have no teeth."

140 A Guide to Children's Spelling Development

Draft

Written by a grade 4 student.
One morning Jim woke up and saw a beanstalk then he climbed up the beanstalk. When he got to the top he saw a castle and said, "I'm hungry. I'll ask the castle for breakfast. I hope they have cornflakes." So Jim runs to the door and knocks. The giant answers, "I used to eat little boys for breakfast, but you (are) safe. Come in." Jim gets some breakfast. "Is your name Jack?" said the giant. "No, my name is Jim," said Jim. "Jack took most of my gold; my gold harp and my magic hen," said the giant. "I wasn't very happy after that. I can't read poetry because of my eyes," said the giant. "Don't you have glasses?" said Jim. "Get me some!" yelled the giant! So the giant gave Jim a gold coin and Jim got the giant glasses. Then the giant said he wanted...

Written by a grade 4 student, retelling a story read to class by the teacher.

Because of the number of misspellings, one could guess that words like *beanstalk, cornflakes, castle, morning, giant* were copied from charts in the classroom or other students. Note these words occur at the beginning of the passage when, perhaps, more attention was given to spelling.

- many common as well as unfamiliar words are constructed using phonics, but not effectively; the unusual letter combinations (**dowre, uenst**) and the misspellings of sight words, **sum** (*some*), **cum** (*come*), **hav** (*have*), indicate this student could improve by using visual strategies. The student relies on phonics, **wos** (*was*), **thay** (*they*), **seid** (sometimes spelled correctly, *said*), **woted** (*wanted*)
- aware of short-vowel sounds, **ar, or,** consonant blends

Suggestions

- review phonics skills: check long-vowel patterns, diphthongs, **r**-influenced vowels and the sound of /**y**/
- develop sight word base: teach visualization and proofreading skills, and an independent study method
- focus on words and discuss common spelling patterns, both in and out of the writing context. Have the student find patterns and sort words according to patterns

Summary

When assessing writing samples, remember to not focus only on the incorrect spellings. It is important to notice the number of correctly spelled words. Remember both correctly and incorrectly spelled words indicate what children are effectively using to construct spellings. As well, remember that assessing spelling in one written product, especially the first draft, does not give the complete picture about children's progress and ability. Observing the process and talking with children about their spelling provides essential information. It is important to examine their spelling over a period of time.

This book has provided a guide to children's spelling development. What children can or cannot spell at a particular age is not paramount. What you need to ensure is that growth is occurring and competency is increasing. Understanding more about this developmental process and how to view children's writing will enable you to help your children continue to develop spelling skills.

NOTES

Appendix A

Growing and Learning: Focus on Writing

In attempting to write, children learn about writing. Learning to write is a by-product of writing for a purpose.

With any finished writing, whether it is a story, poem, essay, recipe or report, the tracks of the process are lost. What is not seen is the great deal of time and effort expended during the process to do the following:

- Come up with ideas
- Begin to put them in words
- Make changes to ideas and words
- Find the best form and the most effective words
- Consider how to formulate ideas and language based on the chosen audience
- Ensure correct grammar, spelling and good organization

Often all this is forgotten when the finished product is read. It all looks so neat and correct. What is it that children need to learn in becoming skilled authors?

Transforming Thought into Writing

Learning to express ideas in writing involves learning about:

Sense of authorship and voice

Children need to think of themselves as writers and develop their own way of stating their points of view. This corresponds to their own voice and style as writers.

Purpose of writing

Children need to realize that writing is done for a variety of purposes (to inform, persuade, entertain, create, analyze, describe, explain, etc.)

In writing to express themselves, children write about what they do, what is important to them, what they think and feel about a variety issues.

In writing to inform others, children need to use the language of reports, instructions, manuals, forms, recipes, timetables, and so on. Children learn that accuracy, clarity and organization are important.

In writing literature, children learn that writing transmits ideas, stories and thoughts designed to have an impact on the reader, to convey a mood and tone, and to elicit responses from the reader.

Focus on an idea, topic or message

By attempting to write, often, children need to learn how to generate and choose topics or ideas. As well, they learn how to limit or expand the content.

Sense of Audience

Children need to understand that the form and language of writing differ according to the intended audience. Writing a letter to a friend calls for a different approach than to an acquaintance, a relative, a business or a newspaper.

Style—The Use of Original and Imaginative Language

Children need to learn how to use words to create tone and mood, to persuade, to inform, to describe, and to elicit specific responses. The use of sentence structure and organization of ideas in written language is different from spoken language.

Structure and Forms of Writing

Children need to learn about the following:

1) The characteristics and formats of fairy tales, mysteries, poetry, essays, novels, letters, journal entries, lists, plays, notes, ads, and so on.

2) The elements of an organized essay (introduction, body, summary)

3) The elements of a story (setting, characters, beginning events leading to climax, endings)

Transcription

Using the conventions of written language, children need to learn printing, handwriting, punctuation, spelling, paragraphing, proofreading, publishing and, with computers being more available, word processing.

Use of Illustrations, Pictures, Diagrams, Figures and Tables

To help clarify and enhance their writing, children need to learn when illustrations, diagrams, figures, pictures and tables should be used and how to effectively structure them.

How Teachers are Helping Children Write

To facilitate effective learning, teachers:

1) Create a positive, comfortable environment in which children can explore their own ideas, grow in confidence, and enjoy and value writing.

2) Provide models of writing by having children listen to, as well as read and discuss, the works of talented authors. In this way, children hear and become aware of the language of literature, sense of story, effective use of language, variety of purposes and extensive powerful vocabulary.

3) Plan activities based on the children's interests and needs. From these experiences, children gain knowledge about the world and language, develop questions for further exploration, and find purposes for writing that are related to their own interests and needs.

4) Provide an environment and opportunities for frequent writing. It is important that both materials and time are available for daily writing. Research into the process that authors use in writing, indicate that children should be encouraged to focus on their writing after some prewriting activities. These could include discussion, brainstorming, webbing, field trips, listening to a speaker or story, or talking with others. During this prewriting time, children decide on a possible focus for writing. They are then encouraged to write their ideas on paper as a first draft. This means the writing is not finished. Children are encouraged in this first draft to focus on getting the ideas down before they forget them. In later drafts, the writing is revised with

the intent to improve the power of the language and organization of ideas. In still later drafts, the conventions of publishing are focused on: spelling, capitalization, punctuation and organization on the page. This is not to say these things are ignored earlier, it is just that gathering ideas and putting language down are the first priorities and perfecting the mechanics comes later. Naturally, not all writing will go to the published stage.

5) Create opportunities for children to share their writing. The purpose of most writing is to inform, persuade, explain, direct and entertain others. Without an audience, much writing has no extended purpose. Thank you letters or requests may be written, invitations sent, announcements and posters put up. Stories may be published in classroom books or displayed on bulletin boards. Writing samples are sent home. Children read their writing to others in their class or other classes and receive feedback. An established audience helps children focus their writing from the very first draft.

6) Finally, teachers explain and model writing skills in class lessons or during writing conferences with children. By watching children when they write and analyzing their writing, teachers can decide what needs to be taught to the class or an individual to help them take the next step.

How Parents Can Help Children with Writing

1) Be aware that writing skills develop slowly. For some children it comes early, while for others it develops later. Occasionally children's skills seem to regress. This is a natural part of learning. For example, when children first become aware of apostrophes, they use them everywhere. Similarly, words they used to spell correctly may now be misspelled. Remember, children use what they know to learn more and to write what they can. With encouragement and sensitive guidance, children progress over the years. Keeping samples of your children's writing will help you and them become aware of their unfolding abilities.

2) Realize that there needs to be preliminary activity and thought before the actual writing. Authors do not sit down and write because someone else asked them to. In helping your child, the following

are important precursors or pre-writing activities:

a) Experiences—the source of ideas, thoughts, knowledge, questions

b) Talking—Explaining, discussing, and expressing their own ideas develops vocabulary

c) Listening—to others' ideas, to stories read aloud; this develops vocabulary and a sense of written language

d) Watching—seeing others write for real-life purposes, noticing the process and effort

3) Encourage frequent writing opportunities

a) Provide materials and a place to write

b) Take time to write with your child

c) Encourage your child to write letters to family members, notes, lists, diary entries, invitations, and so on

d) Share occasions when you get a letter or need to write letters, reminders, notes

e) Keep samples of writing so progress can be seen over the years

4) When your child is writing:

a) Talk through their ideas, have them draw first, dramatize some ideas and/or discuss what and how to say it.

b) Answer their questions about spelling, vocabulary use and punctuation as they write. Encourage them to put down their ideas as well as they can, using their best spelling. This means spelling the words they know and constructing the spelling of less familiar words using what they know.

c) When proofreading or revising, work with them. Have them find words, sentences, ideas and spellings to change. Focus on only a few items at a time. Remember, the errors indicate both what is known and what has not yet been learned.

d) Be interested primarily in content, what matters most are the ideas and how they are presented.

e) Point out the features of the writing that show improvement, that are effective in expressing ideas, and that are novel, interesting or exciting.

f) Indicate what the writing means to you and provide positive encouragement.

5) When reading your children's finished writing, respond to the content, message, ideas and thoughts as you would respond to an adult's writing. Answer, if it is a request; laugh, if it is a joke; ask questions, if it is explaining; comment on your feelings, if it is expressing issues and concerns; comment on the knowledge, if it is informing. In other words, respond with genuine interest.

Writing is connected to all language learning and emerges from children listening, talking, reading, experiencing and playing in interaction with children, adults and language. As other language and communication skills develop and grow, so do writing skills, given a fostering environment and guidance from more experienced and understanding authors.

Appendix B

Words that can be Used to Teach Phonetic, Sounding-Out, and Word-Analogy strategies

Note: Under each category below examples of words are given. Each list can be expanded by using words that rhyme with those in the list for example, in the short /ā/ list *cat* is given, however, other words could be *hat, bat, mat, fat, sat,* and so on. In the short /ō/ list *mop* is given. Rhyming words such as *top, pop, slop stop* could be used.

Activities to use with these words:

1. Print words on cards. Play "fish" card games.

    For example, "Do you have a word that rhymes with *cat*?" or "Do you have a word that has the /ā/ sound as in *fan*.

2. Have your child try to spell a few words in a short sentence, for example, *The cat hops on the bed.*

3. Play rhyming games. "I am thinking of a word that rhymes with bed." You or your child has to guess the word.

4. Draw pictures of the words on cards, then sort them according to vowel sounds and consonant sounds. (see p. 150)

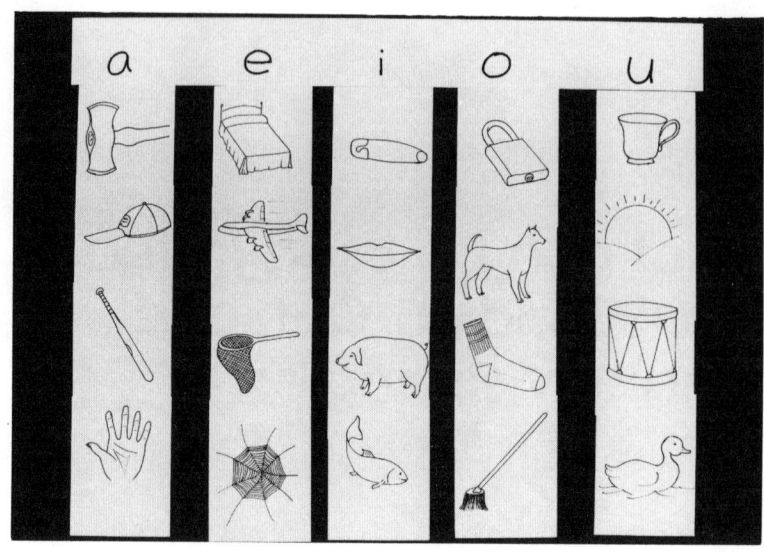

Consonants and Short Vowel Sounds
Words Having 1 Letter to 1 Sound Relationships
(remember the lists can be expanded by using rhyming words.

a as in *a*pple	o as in *o*ctopus	i as in *i*t	u as in *u*p	e as in *e*lephant
cat	dog	hit	fun	ten
has	mop	big	cup	red
mad	hot	him	bug	get
fan	fox	is	cut	sent
and	job	sip	bus	end
flag	hop	six	just	rest
ask				

Generally children find it easiest to learn the vowel sounds in the order of ***a, o, i, u, e.***

Appendix B 151

Help children feel the differences in articulation (what the mouth and tongue do when making the sounds).

For words with *ef, el, em, en, es, ex*, it is difficult to hear the /e/ sound. You can explain that if they hear the letter name *f, l, m, n, s, x* then put *ef, el, em, en, es, ex*: *left, help, them, send, best, next*.

Some mnemonic devices to help in remembering the vowel sounds:

a as in apple

o as in octopus or as in "Aw, can't I stay up late?"

i children learn the word *it* quite easily—so **i** as in *it* will help them.

u as in up (The baby doesn't speak properly but says /u/ instead of up. The arms form the letter u.)

e as in bed or as in elephant

Consonant blends, digraphs and double consonants
(along with vowel sounds and consonant sounds)

r blends	l blends	s blends	prenasal consonants	digraphs
crab	clap	scat	jump	crush
crash	clam	skin	trump	chop
drop	plum	skip	spend	chat
drum	plan	slam	sand	much
grab	flag	slot	hint	lunch
grin	flop	smell	went	when
brag	glum	snip		whip
brass	glad	snap		this
trip	sled	spot		that
trap	slip	spin		thump
frog		stop		with
frost		stamp		path
		swim		shop
		fast		shut
		list		fish

Other consonant combinations

ng nk	ll ff	ss ck	pt ct
sang	spill	glass	kept
thing	shell	cress	swept
long	full	miss	adopt
hung	hall	cross	act
bank	doll	back	inspect
rink	cliff	pick	expect
trunk	off	trick	
bunk	cuff	lock	
		puck	

Because **qu** sounds like **cw**, children need to relate this sound to the letters **qu**, rather than trying to sound it out: *quit, quiz, quack, queen*.

Long Vowel Patterns
(remember to expand list by using rhyming words)

Long a /ā/ a_e ay ai		Long e /ē/ ee ea e y ey		Long i /ī/ i_e y igh ind ild		Long o /ō/ o_e oa ow old ost o		
make	day	tree	me	time	by	home	boat	bold
name	say	sleep	be	ride	my	rode	load	gold
made	may	green	she	mile	why	woke	goal	ghost
gave	play	feed	he	five	night	hope	loan	most
place	rain	teeth	baby	like	light	bone	oar	go
ate	train	meet	happy	nine	find	chose	show	so
case	nail	feel	funny	life	kind	note	grow	no
page	wait	eat	hockey	rise	mild	drove	blow	
		read	monkey	fire	child			
		dear		mice				
		team		bite				
		deal						
		mean						

Long u /ū/ u_e ew oo ue		-ck versus -ke		adding e to cvc words	
mule	new	rack	rake	quit	quite
rule	few	shack	shake	us	use
huge	boo	pick	like	rob	robe
fume	pool	trick	hike	tap	tape
use	soon	lock	spoke	tub	tube
cute*	room	shock	woke		
cube*	true	duck	duke		
cure*	glue	luck			

*cū sounds like letter name q

Vowel Diphthongs and Other Patterns

ow	ou	oy oi	oo	aw	au
how	house	boy	cool	draw	caught
down	out	toy	spoon	saw	sauce
owl	our	coin	moo	lawn	daughter
grow	south	boil	good	yawn	
show	soup	point	look		
	bought	noise			
		choice			

al	wa	ea		y	
		long **e**	short **e**	long **i**	long **e**
always	water	meat	head	sky	candy
salt	was	read	ready	cry	party
ball	want	team	weather	spy	muddy
also	walk			my	penny

R-Influenced Vowels

ar	or	er	ir	ur
car	for	term	girl	hurt
farm	pork	serve	bird	turn
start	sport	sister	shirt	fun
shark	storm	other	first	church
hard	corn	over	dirt	purse
sharp	north	after	birth	
	porch		stir	

R-Influenced Vowels (Continued)

air	are	ear	ear	wor	ear	eer
/ar/ sound			/er/ sound		/er/ sound	
pair	wear	earth		work	dear	
chair	bear	early		world	fear	
stair	pear	search		worth	cheer	
share	tear	learn		worst	deer	
scare				worm		

Silent Letters

l	k	w	t	b	h	gh
half	knee	write	often	comb	ghost	night
walk	know	wrong	castle	thumb		thought
false	knit	wrap	listen	doubt		caught

Adding Endings

	cvc	cvcc	cvvc	cve	y	ay, ey, oy
ing	running getting	jumping helping	meeting boiling	racing baking	carrying trying	playing enjoying
ed	pa**tt**ed rob**b**ed	crashed printed	looked headed	raked taped	fried tried	played enjoyed
er	red**d**er big**g**er	taller hunter	greener cleaner	riper cuter	happ**i**er health**i**er	-
est	thin**n**est mad**d**est	fastest grandest	cleanest greenest	ripest cutest	funn**i**est slopp**i**est	-
s/es	cats dogs	parks plants	blooms sheets	kites homes	carries candies	turkeys plays toys

Adding s to words ending with

ch sh	ss x	z	f (depends on pronunciation)	
matches	guesses	buzzes	knife - knives	chief - chiefs
churches	misses	fizzes	leaf - leaves	roof - roofs
wishes	foxes		elf - elves	cliff - cliffs
splashes	mixes		belief - believes - beliefs	

Adding ed:

—sounds like

/ed/ after **d t**	/t/ after **s p x k f** **ch sh ce**	/d/ after other consonants	
landed	dressed	huffed	spelled	grabbed
weeded	slipped	launched	grinned	sprayed
planted	mixed	fished	groomed	spoiled
acted	liked	raced	cared	begged
	kicked	danced	loved	fizzed

Other Letter Sequences and Sounds

Hard consonant	Soft consonant	Compare sounds of -**se** and -**ce**
c sounds like /**k**/ **g** sounds like /**g**/ when followed by **a o u**	**c** sounds like /**s**/ **g** sounds like /**j**/ when followed by **i e y**	
cat game cot goat cut gum	city giant cent gentle fancy gym	noi**se** ra**ce** chee**se** offi**ce** no**se** dan**ce**

i before **e** except after **c**, or when it sounds like /ā/ as in weigh

field	re**c**eive	neighbour
chief	**c**eiling	vein
niece	de**c**eive	eight

ph, gh can sound like **f**   **ph**one   cou**gh**
                                        gra**ph**   lau**gh**
                                          ele**ph**ant   enou**gh**

i can say /ē/ in the endings of words:

India	curious	beautiful	radio	happier
funniest	medium	radial	radical	Columbian

Multisyllabic Words—Patterns

vc· cv (double consonants, different consonants, digraphs)

sud· den	bet· ter	can· dy	cor· ner	moth· er
man· ner	hap· pen	gar· den	doc· tor	bush· el

v· cv (open syllable)　　　**vc· v** (closed syllable)

la· zy	ho· tel	riv· er	can· al
re· port	pi· lot	vis· it	cov· er
pu· pil	pa· per	clev· er	plan· et
e· vent	o· pen	doz· en	lev· el

-le syllables

bu· gle	ti· tle	bot· tle	peb· ble	trem· ble
la· dle	sta· ple	sad· dle	wig· gle	jun· gle
ta· ble	ri· fle	mid· dle	bub· ble	sim· ple

Homophones (Homonyms)*

by—buy—bye	pair—pear	son—sun	sail—sale
eight—ate	steel—steal	eye—I	piece—peace
aunt—ant	which—witch	pain—pane	hear—here
pail—pale	to—too—two	blue—blew	their—there—they're
way—weigh	tail—tale	bear—bare	week—weak
four—for	write—right	through—threw	knew—new

*There are many others, begin to collect them with your children.

Suffixes and Prefixes

Suffixes

-ly	-ful	-ness	-en	-tion	-ture
really	handful	darkness	fasten	question	future
finally	cheerful	weakness	sharpen	station	nature
usually	helpful	sickness	lengthen	vacation	adventure
friendly	powerful	idleness	fallen	addition	picture
likely	thankful	kindness	golden	pollution	pasture
happily	beautiful	silliness	widen	subtraction	capture

-age	-ment	-less	ous/ious	-able
package	payment	hopeless	famous	usable
manage	basement	jobless	dangerous	notable
garbage	settlement	ageless	enormous	enjoyable
village	apartment	priceless	furious	stretchable
bandage	department	worthless	curious	lovable
postage	amazement	penniless	serious	likable

Prefixes

re- (again)	un- (not)	mis- (wrongly)	pre- (before)
return	unclean	misspell	preschool
rewrite	unable	miscue	preplan
repaint	unpack	misname	prepay
refinish	uneven	misprint	preview
reread	untie	misspend	preshrink
redo	unfair	misfortune	predict

NOTES

Appendix C

Frequently Used Words

The 115 most frequently used words that account for about 50% of all words used in reading and writing are given in Table 6 on page 46. Those words are a good place to start with young children. In addition to those, the following 385 words can be focused on as they progress from beginning to more competent reading and writing skills. Remember, children need to be able to read words if they are to spell them correctly. (About 1000 words account for 90% of written language, therefore these 500 account for about 70% of the most frequently written words.)

again	off	every	often	always
back	part	food	old	below
came	read	form	place	between
day	same	give	put	come
end	take	go	right	does
few	under	going	saw	don't
get	want	here	tell	found
help	air	home	think	good
important	along	last	until	great
keep	because	left	us	house
large	children	me	well	line
man	different	men	went	look
name	even	never	also	might

Adapted from: *Increasing Student Spelling Achievement* (1989) Rebecca Sitton, Curriculum Associates Inc.

I'm	change	mother	however	green
together	done	plants	sure	horse
too	enough	play	turned	hot
world	family	several	able	idea
write	group	side	became	inside
around	hand	since	dog	less
asked	it's	took	early	letter
away	knew	top	fast	mean
still	later	toward	gave	notice
such	morning	without	hold	order
above	need	almost	I'll	person
began	only	animals	kept	piece
car	paper	body	learned	ready
didn't	room	boy	matter	really
earth	seen	cut	nothing	remember
face	sentence	during	oh	short
got	today	example	open	show
half	told	five	perhaps	six
kind	usually	hear	ran	space
land	whole	heard	sad	talk
moon	young	high	table	wind
near	against	light	voice	ago
once	better	live	whether	am
page	city	move	yes	among
red	door	point	yet	before
sea	ever	story	add	behind
thing	feet	sun	become	can't
upon	fish	true	draw	certain
white	hard	try	eat	fine
year	head	turn	English	fire
across	learn	answer	feel	ground
best	life	himself	felt	grow

small	front	easy	itself	possible
those	full	fact	lay	power
thought	living	game	least	rock
three	river	happened	pattern	round
through	run	ice	poor	simple
while	stand	job	quite	size
why	start	language	real	sky
work	state	outside	road	snow
another	tree	past	shall	third
any	friend	question	ship	tiny
big	suddenly	rain	themselves	watch
both	summer	sat	warm	weather
must	system	tall	although	bottom
something	within	understand	animal	bring
sound	ten	walk	begin	center
hundred	that's	walked	blue	check
list	though	already	boat	everything
lived	brought	beautiful	carry	follow
probably	built	carefully	centre	foot
rest	common	deep	dry	hour
special	stood	distance	everyone	longer
town	stop	either	finally	low
anything	strong	else	floor	problem
area	complete	fall	gold	someone
black	course	field	gone	stay
book	surface	girl	heavy	wide
box	alone	glass	held	wild
certain	ball	heart	leave	winter
class	care	instead	leaves	build
close	dark	our	new	mixed
should	school	own	number	much
show	set			

Appendix D

One Child's Development Over One Year

One child's entries in her journal over 10 months in her second year of school exemplifies the developmental process and growth described in this book.

Note the progression during this time toward:

- longer journal entries
- larger range of vocabulary that is attempted
- more knowledge about letter-sound relationships
- effective construction of unfamiliar words using phonics knowledge and sounding strategies: *lerd—learned, invitid—invited, frend—friend, pollhit—polite*
- correct spelling of frequently used words indicating developing visual strategies and an increasing bank of easily spelled words: *baby, that, Sunday, how, her,*

mom, fell, birthday, happy, etc.). Note, ***mi*** and ***tes*** (see September) are later spelled ***my*** and ***teeth***

These samples illustrate the value of examining a child's writing over time. It is evident that this child is making progress in both writing and spelling even though not all words are correctly spelled. With frequent writing opportunities, guidance to promote further spelling awareness, and exposure to both written and oral language, this child will continue to expand her competency in written language skills.

September

> Ilike mI tes Draft

I like my teeth.

October

> I pm pcbp cb f he wh ce Draft

I am a cabbage patch doll for halloween.

November

> Yesterbo r I w We nt to GSm Draft

Yesterday I went to Goldstream

January

> I mit BaBY Sit my siF aft r School Draft

I might baby sit myself after school.

February

> I have i a newl by mouse Draft

I have a new toy mouse.
(child received some help with spelling words)

Appendix D

March

My tooth fell out this morning when mom was washing my face.

April

In four days it is going to be my birthday and I'm happy and one of my friends are sleeping over and that's Joanna.

May

One Sunday I was invited to swimming with my friend Sara because her mom thinks I am so nice and polite and I just learned how to swim.

June

In a couple days ago Kyle came over but Sara was there and she was jealous and me and Kyle were the only ones who cleaned up but Sara didn't clean up because Kyle and me cleaned up we ate a cookie and we made a fort and on Saturday it was Victoria Day downtown but I didn't go there but lots of people went to the parade and on Monday I went to Sara's and we watched a movie that they rented and I had to go home just in time.

NOTES

Also available from

Active Learning Institute

Box 6275, Victoria, B.C. V8P 5L5
Phone (604) 477-0105   Fax (604) 477-9105

Spelling Strategies You Can Teach

by Mary Tarasoff
128 pp. soft cover

- Describes the developmental stages of children.
- Explains in detail knowledge and spelling strategies you can teach.
- Presents ideas for assessment, evaluation and instruction in school programs.

$19.95 plus $3.00 (postage & handling) + $1.61 (GST) = **Total $24.56 each**

Alphadeck Card Game

for ages 4 and up

- A new card game using the alphabet and pictures.
- 104 cards, high quality plastic coated in presentation box.
- Includes rules and suggestions for hours of fun for the whole family.

$14.95 plus $3.00 (postage & handling) + $1.26 (GST) = **Total $19.21 each**
B.C. residents please add provincial sales tax